AMERICA THE
EXCEPTIONAL

Praise for Frank Moore
and *America the Exceptional*

"As a veteran FDNY fire fighter who responded to and worked the horrible scene at Ground Zero following the 9/11 attacks, Frank Moore has earned the right and has the insights to address what has gone seriously wrong with America. He also outlines the steps it will take to restore our great nation to the vision of freedom and faith in God embraced by our Founding Fathers. Frank is a devout Christian and a true American patriot, and what he has to say in *America the Exceptional* is exceptionally spot-on!"

— **Dr. Carol Swain,** author, political pundit, former college professor at Princeton and Vanderbilt

"Frank Moore has captured the intentions of the Founding Fathers and their documents that established the standards for America . . . that link "our Creator" to our country's purpose, contrasting their intentions to today. It has been said that heroism is simple and yet rare. Everyone who does the best he can is a hero. But it shines in those that live to protect us . . . the firemen, policemen, servicemen, and all of the first responders. Forgetting the basics of our founding principles will lead our country toward secularism and away from our Creator, destroying America as we have known it."

— **Brig. Gen. R. Dennis Kerr**, USA, Retired

"Frank, thank you for writing this tremendous book, *America the Exceptional.* You have captured the key insights that made America great and presented them in a captivating way. Your book should be read across America. For our nation to preserve its freedoms, we must rediscover its founding secrets, and your book does exactly that. God bless you and your important work."

— **William J. Federer,** American historian and author

"Our nation is 'progressively' heading in the wrong direction, and why wouldn't it be when we put our 'trust in princes' and not Our Creator. Lt. Moore understands this as well as anyone and has taken on this project to do his part in 'righting the ship.' As a leader in the FDNY during the tragic events of 9/11/01, he saw firsthand the brutal unprovoked attack on the United States of America; he also saw the American spirit come alive that tragic day. Today, paying very close attention to the ongoing assaults on 'American Exceptionalism,' Lt. Moore understands that in order to remain 'exceptional,' we as a nation must again first put our trust in God, and then re-embrace core, first-principle values of defending 'life, liberty and the pursuit of happiness . . . ' "
— **Thomas LaPolla**, battalion chief, FDNY

"Lt. Frank Moore is a great American. His service to others as a fire fighter is just one indication of his willingness to sacrifice his physical well-being; he also understands the importance of religion, specifically Christianity, in the founding of the United States, which requires larger sacrifices from us all. It is a sad reflection of our times that people like Frank Moore are harder to find. I trust that his inspiring example and words will motivate at least a few of us to turn back onto the right road."
— **Kishore Jayabalan**, director, Istituto Acton, Rome

AMERICA THE EXCEPTIONAL

Restoring a Wayward Nation's Greatness

LT. FRANK MOORE, FDNY Ret.

ISBN: 978-0-578-54722-0

Cover design by 360 Media Group
Page layout by Win-Win Words LLC
Cover photo of Ground Zero cross by Anne M. (Bybee) Williams
Author photo by Michael F. Moore

All Scripture quotations, unless otherwise indicated, are taken from the Holy Catholic Bible, Douay Rheims Edition, copyright 2006 by Catholic Treasures and The Ignatius Catholic Study Bible, Revised Standard Version, Second Catholic Edition, copyright 2010 by Ignatius Press, San Francisco.

Printed in the United States of America

To the Holy Spirit,
without whom I would be able to say nothing.
Also, to my wife, Dara, and my whole family, who patiently
supported me throughout the writing of this book.

"If you are on the wrong road, progress means doing an about-turn and walking back to the right road; and in that case the man who turns back soonest is the most progressive man."
— **C. S. Lewis**

CONTENTS

INTRODUCTION

R ECENTLY, I VISITED SCRANTON, PENNSYLVANIA. Memorial walls outside of a government building in downtown Scranton had been erected to honor our soldiers, and the walls displayed quotes from soldiers and famous people, including Gandhi. One of the quotes my wife and I read as we walked from wall to wall was, "Greater love has no man than this, that a man lay down his life for his friends."

Most of us will recognize this quote as the words of Jesus Christ recorded in John 15:13. Shockingly, though, instead of crediting the words to Christ, the attribution 'Anonymous' was beneath the quote and that, of course, is a lie. Yet, besides the fact that this is not an anonymous quote, what was the motivation for labeling it as such? What's the problem in giving credit for the words to their true author, Jesus?

This book is not meant to be an intellectual exercise suitable only for a small audience of academics. It is a sincere exposé for all Americans. I discuss why America must change course, not simply to ensure prosperity for the next generation, but, most importantly, to preserve freedom. In the years since the terrorist attacks of September 11, 2001,

American self-doubt has surfaced, fueled by harsh criticism of our founding. Our country has replaced her original purpose—the protection of God-given individual liberty—to pursue a destructive path that leads to a cold, cynical secularism. The Founding Fathers understood us to be a nation our Creator was involved in creating.

For freedom's sake, America has to change course and return to the ideas from which she was born. That change cannot occur unless we citizens acknowledge the Creator as author of our rights just as our forefathers did. By contrasting our founding with the present day, it will be obvious what makes America unique in the family of nations and what truly makes America great.

To properly select public officials, we must be well-informed but not only about current events. When evaluating our political candidates, it is more important than ever to know the difference between right and wrong, truth and lie, so that America never compromises the self-evident truths she is called to defend. Every time I remember the lives of the 343 firefighters who died at Ground Zero, in New York City, I am reminded not just of the price paid for liberty, but also how it has been paid over and over by every generation and must continue to be paid.

If we are deprived of good information, we select leaders blindly, and if we are ignorant of timeless truth, we act without wisdom. During my research for this book, I started to see that the founders were driven by more than just principle; they had a shared religious experience that they wished to be passed on to subsequent generations. They acknowledged the Creator's participation in their struggle. They also recognized, with humility, that they had been given the blessings they enjoyed. Now it's our duty, if we are to ensure liberty for future generations, to hear their voices and make sure that we diligently seek and defend truth, regardless of the cost. That is the only way to correctly identify current and future threats to freedom.

Information today is shared at a blinding pace, which is why it can be a daunting task to try to make sense of the virtual waterfall of news thrown at us each day. One thing is certain: An exorbitant amount of energy is spent categorizing Americans, whether by race, religion, gender, sexual orientation, or class, with the negative effect of pitting us against ourselves. If all men are created equal, then what purpose do these categories serve? As the song says, "United We Stand, Divided We Fall." A perfect example is the use of the term *middle class* in politics and media. Americans, contrary to popular opinion, shouldn't be characterized by income. We should be recognized by what we contribute. In fact, sometimes the most valuable people among us are very often the least compensated, such as the social worker or the emergency medical technician (EMT). Our income does not thrust us into a class . . . we are not worth less because we earn less. No one takes a job believing they will never see a raise or a promotion. In a free society, incomes are not fixed, but fluid. We know the harder we work, the more we earn.

I hate the term *class* in regard to income. *Classes* aptly describe the sorry state in Socialist and Communist regimes, where a central authority dictates what you are worth. Free people, by contrast, are only limited by themselves because they can fully utilize their unique talents. That's why it is important to recognize what true freedom is and acknowledge why it must be defended.

Contrasting early American thought to that of today, and being objective about it, exposes two different philosophies of life: one is God-focused and the other is man-focused. The Judeo-Christian tradition so often acknowledged in early America, and discounted today, is the heart of human virtue and American Exceptionalism. Moreover, a deeper look into the words of the Founding Fathers shows men soberly acknowledging divine aid in their cause, a point important to consider as we search for the source of American Exceptionalism.

Hard-working Americans have suffered the most as America loses its moorings. Yet it is they who are appealed to in every political campaign. The defining principle that all men are created equal, for which we fought a revolution, is the principle that also defines our freedom. The American Exceptionalism that we wish for our children depends less on democracy than it does to our loyalty to the God of our fathers. The present generation is being taught to abandon transcendent Truth in favor of the oxymoron *relative truth*, and those fighting that trend are under assault.

From the earliest moments of recorded history, people have tried to make sense of the physical world. Living things are immediately distinguished from inert matter, with Man alone possessing intellect. Our shared humanity, human life itself, should foster solidarity between us because of our shared nature. But that nature is divided into physical and spiritual components. The fact that we can disregard all that unites us as creatures and, in spite of that natural solidarity, still do harm to each other, is proof of the existence of good and evil, and clearly exposed by Judeo-Christian tradition.

Mankind seeking exceptionality in this physical world has been led to a spiritual explanation of life and of good and evil. But it was not until God Himself, in the person of Jesus Christ, spoke to all mankind that the whole truth was made clear concerning our solidarity, our dependence on a good God, and the existence of evil. Of all the nations that have ever existed on Earth, only America has had the privilege of being born to reflect this truth. Only America, through its Declaration of Independence, identifies the solidarity of the human race with the Will of God, her Creator. Our Declaration became the perpetual 'monkey on the back' of our government, from the founders on, until slavery was abolished, and it remains the compass guiding us into the future.

Before the American nation was born, her heroes were. Our identity as a people is deeply connected to our forefathers, who fought for our independence. American citizens, cognizant of our ancient heroes, should have a sense of pride because heroism is deeply etched in our history by men and women who rose above history. Just as appropriate is a sense of gratitude for what has been passed on by men who wished to give us their posterity and what they cherished—freedom. Our real American Exceptionalism is in a shared spirit of solidarity. Our exceptionalism as a nation rests on our defending the truth that the value of the individual is determined by God, not Man. The danger today is in forgetting what is different about America. And if we mistakenly confuse American Exceptionalism with a birthright rather than as a defense of the "self-evident" truths, we cannot and will not be exceptional. America is exceptional only if we continue to defend individual liberty as a gift from God. Aleksandr Solzhenitsyn said:

> "... Truth eludes us if we do not concentrate with total attention on its pursuit. And even while it eludes us, the illusion still lingers of knowing it and leads to many misunderstandings."[1]

America the Exceptional

In my years as a New York City fireman, I witnessed heroic acts performed by ordinary people. I have also seen and experienced fear, and I have watched people either rise above or succumb to that fear. It is a telling observation to watch people who forgo their training and, in a panic, do the opposite of what they were taught, often with horrible results, and contrast them with those people who, in similar crises, calmly act according to protocol, able to improvise when necessary, and persevere through adversity. They inspire those around them both through accomplishment and character. Conversely, you can't underestimate what fear can do to judgment. Today, preoccupied with terrorism and security, we should be greatly concerned with the treatment of true heroes in America because they demonstrate and protect freedom and virtue.

My education as a boy subtly connected me to the Founding Fathers. Their respect for Christian beliefs left no doubt in my mind that they served truth and justice. This is in stark contrast to current trends in education. While not universal, it is safe to say that education is not fostering that connection anymore. Instead, it is often trivializing or ignoring our magnificent history and, in some cases, connecting our rise to dishonorable pursuits. George Washington's birthday, rather than celebrated as it was in the past, is forgotten. In the same way, there is a modern popular movement that denies our Christian roots while simultaneously pursuing a path to secularism. The end result is diminished freedom because we are living life in a far different way than we did in the past. If the transcendent standard of Judeo-Christian tradition is removed, then the new standard will be man-made, encouraging all of us to sit in judgment over one another. The Bill of Rights is proof that the founders were single-minded

about our individual liberty; today, however, those efforts are
no longer sufficient. The NSA scandal and the IRS scandal
highlight many events suggesting diminishing freedom in de-
fiance of the Bill of Rights.

It is critical that we pull off the blanket hiding America's
heroes so that their bold actions can return to plain view. We
need to both see them in action and discover what motivates
them. It is not genetic superiority but spiritual strength that
collectively emerges from the human family to make an exceptional people. Exceptional men and women come in many
shapes and sizes, with the common denominator being self-
sacrifice. If we can admit that self-sacrifice is best modeled
after Jesus Christ Himself, we will be well on our way to re-
covering the exceptionalism of those who built this country.
The sad reality is that secularism and freedom are like oil and
water—they do not mix. The Christian worldview that stim-
ulated the action of the Revolution also produced the greatest
nation in history—great not just because of her power, but
also because of her general happiness realized through real
freedom. People from other shores, deprived of personal as-
pirations, abandoned their homes to pursue happiness here,
making America a melting pot.

The connection between freedom and exceptionalism
has been realized throughout our history. America defended
individual liberty, and she benefited from the unimpeded
dreams and hopes of her citizens by achieving prosperity.
Only the foolish would deny the lessons of history demonstrated by our rapid expansion and improved quality of life.
And yet that is precisely what we are doing. If we contrast
America's birth with the rise of Communism, we see a clear
picture of what is at stake. The diminishing freedom and the
economic and political confusion of so-called democratic

Socialism in present-day Europe further demonstrates the danger. Yet Communism, with its trail of death, still thrives because, among other things, it provides a path to domination for those thirsting for power. It will be a hard battle to turn again to the wisdom behind our founding because certain groups, already tasting power, will fight to keep it. They are a growing elite class that distinguishes itself in politics, business, education, and media, and who benefit from the move away from American Exceptionalism.

If a younger generation of Americans, with a healthy skepticism, full of energy, knowing what energized the Founding Fathers, is inspired by this book to get in the fray, we will have taken the first step to restoring exceptionalism. But our Constitution and, more importantly, the principles in the Declaration of Independence, are being whittled away, and there is not a lot of time left.

I want to impress upon every American that this country is not the same place in which I grew up. Although I knew the physical threat of the Cold War, I felt far more secure in my freedom. The colonists had to fight for freedom, and you are in a similar fight. It is a time for new heroes. I quote the well-known Chuck Norris, famous actor and six-time-unde-feated World Professional Middleweight Karate Champion—and the first man from the Western Hemisphere in the more than 4,500-year tradition of Tae Kwon Do to be awarded an eighth-degree black belt—who said:

> "As a young man, I discovered the power of doing hard things. Abject poverty, a father's alcoholism and desertion of our family, and my own shyness were a few of the obstacles I faced and overcame growing up. My mother always told me, 'God has a plan for your life.' And she's right.

Introduction

Each of us is called to reach for greatness. There really is a hero in all of us. We've all been designed by God to be a blessing to many—a hero to some."[2]

This is hard work, but together we will get it done!

— Lieutenant Frank Moore, FDNY retired

"The Americans are the first people whom Heaven has favored with an opportunity of deliberating upon and choosing the forms of government under which they should live."[3]
— **John Jay,**
signer of the Declaration of Independence

AMERICA THE
EXCEPTIONAL

PART I
THE
SUPREME
SACRIFICE

1

WHAT IS EXCEPTIONAL?

"... There is a world of difference between an authority on which you rely when it pleases you, and one which you trust absolutely whether it pleases you or not; for what the world needs is a voice that is right not when the world is right, but right when the world is wrong." [1]
— **Fulton J. Sheen**

I WAS TELLING A FRIEND OF MINE, A CATHOLIC PRIEST FROM INDIA, a story about a West Point cadet who was arguing with me about religion. When I had mentioned the miracles of Jesus, the cadet described the miracles attributed to Krishna. He said Krishna was seen levitating, flying across the sky, and in two places at once. The priest, who was Indian, was smiling and said, "There is no written record of that; families merely pass down stories to their children." Laughing, I told him, "It really doesn't matter, does it? All you have to do to see the difference is look at the miracles. If I'm lying in the road dying of leprosy and two guys come by and one guy flies across the sky and the other guy heals me of my disease, which miracle do you think I'm going to like better?" He laughed loudly.

An analogy can be made between the leper and the American colonies. The leper was overwhelmed by what Jesus did because he recognized that it was done specifically for him. Similarly, our founders knew their victory was won through more than simply the motivation of a just cause.

This is not intended to be a historical piece or a research project; others have already done that. Rather, I want to prove that our ancestors experienced miraculous help and that, just as the leper, they knew they were indebted to God for their cherished liberty. The Declaration of Independence states God created us to be free, which assumes there is a purpose for our freedom and working toward that purpose is American Exceptionalism. What promotes exceptionalism? Conversely, what hinders it? If we allow ourselves to look at the beginning of America as a spiritual event, exceptionalism fits naturally; after all, what else can we expect from God? Today, Christianity is being expelled from the public square, and Christians are being challenged as they exercise their religious beliefs. American Exceptionalism itself is a collection of individual exceptionalism made possible by our Christian heritage.

Is it important to believe in American Exceptionalism? Is it just an expression of idealistic pride or is it, at its heart, the realization of mankind's God-given freedom, freedom which when defended and lived out, is the source of great good? I hope to impress upon you not merely the religiousness of our founding generation but also how they saw God in the history they were about to make.

I have seen exceptionalism throughout my career. With firefighting comes an understanding of the physical danger that goes with it. For this reason, few jobs have a larger cross-section of courageous people than the New York City Fire Department (FDNY), simply because anyone who applies for the job is aware of the dangers, beforehand, that they will experience. They choose to sacrifice their own safety to protect others.

As I approached Ground Zero, the twin towers now missing from the New York skyline, my company and I were not concerned with a lost symbol of American prosperity. We were concerned with all the innocent men, women, and children in the collapse zone and what we could do. At the command post in lower Manhattan, I was joined by hundreds of other firefighters. We did not link the tragedy with an America in decline; we were just thinking, *Let's get in there and help.* As always, the fire department was concerned about saving lives. It was time to do our duty!

To answer the question "What is exceptional?" we must first look at the origin of America. With unsurpassed power and wealth distinguishing America from the rest of the world for decades, it is understandable that Americans might confuse exceptionalism with American military and economic might; they confuse the process with the result. But today, there is a growing sense that we are no longer distinguishing ourselves, that the rest of the world is closing the gap, and that our future absolutely depends on our restoring our superiority. Slogans such as "Make America Great Again,"[2] which hit a popular nerve with the American public, depict general uneasiness about our current course. Yet, aren't we mistaking American Exceptionalism with the *impact* of exceptionalism? Were we not, in fact, exceptional before we achieved superpower status, before we amassed great wealth, and before we became the leader of the free world?

When I examine my life, when I think about all the exceptional people I met in my years as a firefighter, and when I remember what I saw on the days, weeks, and months following the terrorist attacks of 9/11, I see a connection between duty and exceptionalism. Accordingly, to understand exceptionalism, you must also get to the root of what inspires a sense of duty. Not many firefighters would label themselves brave, yet there are many brave firefighters. To recognize bravery's importance, we must know what it is. Bravery is not the absence of fear. Rather, it is doing one's duty in spite of it. Throughout the NYC Fire Department's history, a culture of bravery has developed, inspiring the next generation of firefighters to continue the tradition. A new group comes along to replace the old, ignoring personal risk in the performance of their duty. The characteristics seen in the NYC Fire Department provide us with a microcosm of what makes America exceptional.

Today, national anxiety is indicative of a change from the course set by our ancestors. It is seen in the obsessive need to categorize us rather than to see us all as Americans. The result is a forgotten sense of mission and an America on a new path to mediocrity. So, the question is: "What marks the old path?" An unbiased foreign observer, Alexis De Tocqueville, hit upon the key to America's freedom. He made this observation in the 1830s concerning religion's positive influence on our country:

"On my arrival in the United States, the religious aspect of the country was the first thing that struck my attention; and the longer I stayed there, the more I perceived the great political consequences resulting from this new state of things. In France I had almost always seen the spirit of religion and the spirit of freedom marching in opposite directions. But in America I found they were intimately united and that they reigned in common over the same country."[3]

What Is Exceptional?

The religious aspect of the country Tocqueville saw was unmistakably Christian, and the confidence which we once had came from knowing what is right. That produced both the will to defend liberty and the fuel for exceptionalism. In the same way the sacrificial mission of fire departments in general is inspired by the mission of America, the mission of America is inspired by Christian principles.

Searching for victims at Ground Zero after the collapse of the World Trade Center, I descended through the rubble with my company. I was squeezing through a sea of I-beams, rebar, and concrete when Mike (a firefighter under my command) radioed that he found a void. A void is an opening in a collapse where survivors might be. His voice was followed by radio traffic warning of the potential for a secondary collapse. Joining Mike would entail more than simply climbing farther down through the pile (the name given to the collapsed World Trade Center). It required sliding down snake-like through the debris with little consideration given to how I might find my way back out. The tight quarters and warnings of secondary collapse were easily dismissed because of our duty toward each other and the victims. So, finally, I found a large empty space forty feet below that I believe was part of a subway station. There were no victims there. Looking at seven floor joists crammed into that small space, I began to realize that it would take a miracle for anybody to have survived. Undeterred, we all continued to hope, tirelessly searching for signs of life. The dedication of the firefighters that day is a small-scale version of the American people's brave dedication to liberty throughout her history, and that commitment to liberty is the byproduct of a Christian founding that defends human dignity. Americans rightly attest to cultivating a culture of bravery, one of the many byproducts of exceptionalism.

The truth is that the early Americans, our forebears, risked everything, including their lives, not for wealth and power but to gain and preserve liberty for themselves and for their posterity. Every battle fought, every hardship endured, had this as its goal. Our generation must resolve in a similar way to preserve that liberty for our posterity. *A free country* is what our forebears won. It was not a victory for rich society or for any of the wealth and power to which we have become accustomed. Those are merely the fruits of real freedom that are rooted in the Christian sense of duty.

The founders declared, "We hold these truths to be self-evident, that all men are created equal . . . " That self-evident truth is really not that self-evident. Our belief in equality stems from our belief that human beings are created and that our value must necessarily be determined by the Creator. That belief also compels us to defend the freedom of every person. Equality, as understood by the founders, is not, however, self-evident once we deny the Creator as the source of that truth. Without the Creator, we are simply a different country.

" . . . Truth eludes us if we do not concentrate with total attention on its pursuit. And even while it eludes us, the illusion still lingers of knowing it and leads to many misunderstandings."[4] (Aleksandr Solzhenitsyn)

The Declaration of Independence gives purpose to our Constitution because the Creator, recognized by the founders in the Declaration, defines us as equals. This truth, so obvious it was deemed self-evident, is an enemy to the power hungry, and there lies the danger of our progression to secularism; it replaces the authority of the Creator with that of Man.

Who was the Creator to the Founding Fathers, and what did they actually mean by the word *religion*? Those questions are germane to the discussion about American Exceptionalism. Some in the intelligentsia are advancing the notion that the founders were deists. If true, it would mean the founders did not believe that the Creator intervened in the affairs of men.[5] This is contrary to the Christian, who sees the Creator as a participant in the future of the world to the point where He gave His only begotten Son, Jesus Christ. So which Creator is the Creator of our Founding Fathers?

Answering that question will lead us to a better understanding of what makes America exceptional. Two Congressional acts from that time can help answer that question of who the referred-to Creator was and identify a government with a very different philosophy than today's deism. The United States Congress, on September 11, 1777, appropriated money to purchase twenty thousand copies of the Bible. Five years later, on September 10, 1782, the Congress authorized the publishing of an American version of the Bible.[6] The importance of the Bible to the founders of our country gives a clear picture as to who they were and what they believed. These acts of Congress contradict the notion that these men were essentially deists.

"There is nothing . . . we look for with more certainty than this principle, that Christianity is a part of the law of the land. Every thing declares this. The generations which have gone before speak to it, and pronounce it from the tomb. We feel it. All, all proclaim that Christianity, general, tolerant Christianity, is the law of the land."[7] (Daniel Webster)

Although some modern historians like to label them deists, that first government was Christian, and the Declaration of Independence and the Constitution, especially the First Amendment[8], are better understood in light of that fact. It gives us an insight, not just into its original intent but also Christianity's intended role in the new government in order to defend the rights of citizens. Their definition of religion itself is closely related to the Bible as seen in this act of Congress in 1781:

"In 1781, . . . the subject of printing the Bible was again presented to Congress, and . . . referred to a committee of three. The committee . . . recommended to Congress an edition printed by Robert Aitken; whereupon it was 'Resolved, that the United States, in Congress assembled, highly approve the pious and laudable undertaking of Mr. Aitken, as subservient to the interests of religion; and . . . recommend this edition to the inhabitants of the United States.' "[9]

That generation did not foresee the need to define religion but, in light of the conflicts surrounding the First Amendment, it is a necessary discussion.

"The Bill of Rights contains no grant of privilege for a group of people to destroy the Bill of Rights."[10] (Dwight Eisenhower)

Modern battles over religious freedom fail to recognize the role of Christianity to oversee the exercise of that freedom. Christianity is the greatest proponent of individual liberty, and it is individual liberty protected by the Declaration of Independence that draws people from across the globe to America.

"Well-meaning Americans in the name of freedom have taken freedom away. For the sake of religious tolerance, they've forbidden religious practice."[11] (Ronald Reagan)

In order to defend against existential threats to liberty, such as Socialism, Fascism, or Communism, a country must unite behind a common understanding of the equal value of each human being. That premise is at the heart of and uniquely defended by Christianity.

To restore exceptionalism, we must know what it is and visualize it. The founders saw freedom and human rights as gifts from God. And if we are made in His image and likeness, we are free creators here on earth.

"If you perform your part, you must have the strongest confidence that the same Almighty Being who protected your venerable and pious forefathers, who enabled them to turn a barren wilderness into a fruitful field, who so often made bare his arm for their salvation, will be still mindful of you, their offspring."[12] (Joseph Warren)

As we will soon see, God was recognized by the founders as the source of both exceptionalism and freedom. If the founders were correct, when America rejects God, she stifles herself.

"War is first in man, then among men. The conflict on the battlefields is but the extension of the conflict within man. Man revolting against God is the miniature of the war of man revolting against his fellowman."[13] (Fulton Sheen)

The modern revolt against God is separating us from the source of exceptionalism. American government's goal is to protect the "life, liberty, and the pursuit of happiness"[14] of every person, yet the pursuit of happiness should not detract but instead contribute to the happiness of others. American Exceptionalism is perpetuated by Christian doctrine that asks us to help our neighbor.

" . . . we are, by the necessity of preferring and pursuing true happiness as our greatest good, obliged to suspend the satisfaction of our desires in particular cases."[15] (John Locke)

As America abandons God, it is natural that she becomes fearful. Without God, prosperity itself becomes the goal rather than the byproduct of freedom. Post-9/11 America is witnessing the slow erosion of our freedom for the sake of security because without a sense of the eternal, we are left with only the 'now.' Once any particular liberty is sacrificed in the name of security, all liberties are on the table because liberty is no longer cherished above all; self-preservation is.

"It is essential that we should relearn frankly to face the fact that freedom can be had only at a price and, that as individuals, we must be prepared to make severe material sacrifices to preserve our liberty."[16] (F. A. Hayek)

Any reflection on exceptionalism should begin by recalling both the severe material sacrifices of our ancestors and what they believed.

2

THE GREAT SEAL

D URING THE FRENCH AND INDIAN WAR IN JULY 1755, George Washington participated in the Battle of Monongahela with the British forces. It was a devastating defeat, with the British suffering more than 900 killed or wounded out of almost 1,400, as compared to French and Indian losses of about thirty. Every British officer on horseback was either killed or wounded except for George Washington, who wrote of the disaster to his younger brother, John Augustine Washington, on July 18, 1755. He says:

"As I have heard, since my arrival at this place, a circumstantial account of my death and dying speech, I take this early opportunity of contradicting the first, and of assuring you, that I have not as yet composed the latter. But by the All-Powerful Dispensations of Providence, I have been protected beyond all human probability or expectation; for I had four bullets through my coat, and two horses shot under me, yet escaped unhurt, although death was leveling my companions on every side of me!"[1]

Had Washington been killed in this battle more than twenty years before the Revolution, the America we live in today would never have come to exist. As he states to his brother, he was protected and, in the process, so was America!

What role did God play in the emergence of America on the world stage? Honest analysis of what Americans thought from the beginning of our history into the twentieth century indicate that we Americans take much more for granted today than did Americans in the past. There has been, for much of our history, an honest consensus that God favored America. The question is: "Why?"

A few years ago, I attended a lecture given by a former ambassador, Dr. Michael Novak, which was titled "American Exceptionalism." He was speaking at the Acton Institute's "Acton University." The Institute, whose motto, "Power tends to corrupt and absolute power corrupts absolutely," taken from Lord Acton, is dedicated to the study of the free and virtuous society. We all entered the lecture room, people of diverse ages from many different countries, and sat down waiting for Dr. Novak. A man in his eighties, he entered the room walking very slowly with help and was brought to a chair in front of us. Although he was very feeble, his voice was both cheerful and full of conviction as he started to talk about America.

He began by saying, "If everyone has a dollar bill, please take it out and examine the back; on the back is the secret to American Exceptionalism." Everyone began fumbling around, looking for a dollar. The unusual start engaged us immediately. My eyes went first to "In God We Trust" and then several people said it out loud. Dr. Novak shook his head "no" half grinning and said, "Look again." People started guessing until he stopped us and told us to look at the pyramid. The pyramid, he said, held the secret to American Exceptionalism.

He described the pyramid as the symbol of human government throughout history, with the peak representing the ruler. According to Dr. Novak, the peak removed from the base represented the tyrant being removed as governor of the people, exchanged for a new governor, the eye of Providence. The Founding Fathers were acknowledging the true ruler, perfect, unchanging and just, whose laws were not arbitrary. The law of God applied to everyone, including the would-be King. That is how true freedom is accomplished, with laws and government held to standards outside the control of human beings.

That lecture pointed me toward a different explanation of American Exceptionalism. I had previously been focused on the effects of freedom on society, but that didn't seem to be enough. Dr. Novak, however, used the pyramid from the Great Seal of the United States to connect exceptionalism with the Creator. American Exceptionalism was the result of replacing one ruler with another, replacing the tyrant with the perfect lawgiver, God.

I loved this new avenue, but I didn't know anything about the history of the Great Seal of the United States. I kept picturing the Nicolas Cage movie, *National Treasure*, thinking the Seal originated from Freemasonry. I started to research the Seal so I could refer to it myself, and what I discovered made me reconsider what motivated that generation.

What is the difference between religion and a 'religious experience'? Dr. Novak had asked us to look at the back of a one-dollar bill because he wanted us to reflect on what it symbolized. World history to that point had been the story of the tyrant and of power. America changed the story to one of a nation under God.

Yet, they did not intend this to be a sign of the superiority of their beliefs, but rather acknowledgment to God for His help, which they felt obligated to communicate to the world.

The Great Seal (commons.wikimedia.org).

The question is: "What events did they see as miraculous?" Yes, the new 'American pyramid' declares God as sovereign, but its place in America's timeline calls for a closer look at their experiences.

The first thing that struck me as odd was Congress's starting the process on July 4, 1776. That day just seemed too important and the times too perilous to be thinking about a seal or emblem. The idea that Congress would have both the Declaration of Independence and the Great Seal on the same day's agenda seemed strange. The Declaration made sense; after all, we declared war with Great Britain, but what is the necessity for the Seal? I could think of no practical reason for spending time and energy on that with all the challenges of the war. America was not yet a nation. Why were the Founding Fathers expending energy to create a national emblem rather than perhaps recruiting more militia, requisitioning more muskets and cannons, or securing allies? Wouldn't they be consumed with winning the war first? Weren't they putting the cart before the horse? Nevertheless, it was important enough to do on that first Fourth of July, and I knew if I could find out why, it would give me great insight into what they believed.

"Resolved, That Dr. Franklin, Mr. J. Adams, and Mr. Jefferson, be a committee, to bring in a device for a seal for the United States of America."² (July 4, 1776, *Journals of the Continental Congress*)

Let's forget the date for the moment and look at whom Congress gave the task to. Benjamin Franklin, John Adams, and Thomas Jefferson—three of the most respected men of their time, chosen to draft the Declaration of Independence, were again chosen to develop the nation's emblem—immediately after ratifying the Declaration. That emphasizes the seriousness Congress gave to the Seal's message. It doesn't seem logical that they would take on trivial duties at such a serious time. A look at their suggestions will give you insight into their minds.

Franklin suggested an image of Moses, touched by rays from Heaven, standing on the shore extending his hand over the sea as it came down over Pharaoh. Jefferson suggested the same setting, Israel protected from Pharaoh during the Exodus by a pillar of fire. Adams suggested the painting of the "Judgement of Hercules." Interestingly, both Franklin and Jefferson compare America to the Israelites and England to the Egyptians. But, in that analogy, who won the battle for the Israelites? In the Exodus, acknowledged by both Jews and Christians, it was God Himself who defeated Pharaoh. So what does this analogy used by both Franklin and Jefferson have to do with the American Revolution, other than God's miraculous defense of the American cause? The images were complex and all three were rejected! What would Congress finally agree to?

The Continental Congress did not give up. They formed a second committee comprised of James Lovell, John Morin Scott, and William Churchill Houston almost four years later, on March 25, 1780, while still embroiled in an unpredictable war. Their proposal, a shield with thirteen white and red stripes held by a warrior on one side and a figure holding olive branches on the other, presented May 10, was, however, similarly rejected. They were then followed by a third committee of Arthur Middleton, John Rutledge, and Elias Boudinot (later joined by Arthur Lee) on May 4, 1782. Their seal was of an eagle holding the American flag and a shield held by a warrior on one side and a maiden holding a dove on the other. Submitted on May 9, it was also rejected. That is when the third committee gave all three proposals to Charles Thomson, Secretary of the Continental Congress.

I am telling the whole story because I'm trying to impress upon you how important what the emblem actually meant was to the Founding Fathers. They felt compelled to create the Seal immediately after we declared our independence because they were obliged to acknowledge divine help. They were patient and persistent because they wanted to say something specific that would not be mistaken.

The peculiar importance of its stated message is presumed because of the rejections of the previous proposals; otherwise, they would have accepted one of them. Six years passed, and the Congress still had not settled on a seal. But Thomson was successful. Not only that, his design was approved the very same day it was submitted, June 20, 1782. No lengthy deliberation. Secretary Thomson hit the nail on the head, and knowing what made it so appealing will tell us what the country meant to them. The Seal's meaning is not something that needs to be guessed at. Charles Thomson communicated its meaning in an official statement labeled "Remarks and Explanation" that describes the meaning of the images used in the Great Seal.

"The pyramid signifies Strength and Duration: The Eye over it & the Motto allude to the many signal interpositions of Providence in favour of the American cause."[3]

This is what they wanted to say through the Great Seal, precisely and simply. The Founding Fathers were of one accord that, at many critical moments, God had acted on their behalf. The perseverance and attention given to the Great Seal's creation demonstrates that the message behind the Seal was something of peculiar importance to them. For them to begin this project on July 4, 1776—in fact, to begin this project at all while in the middle of the war—makes very clear, not just that they believed God was at work for them, but also that they had to say it to the world.

Connecting the Declaration of Independence to the Great Seal of the United States uncovers what the country was intended to be, a nation under God. Today, as we contemplate how to restore American Exceptionalism, we should begin by considering what put us on the path to exceptionalism.

"The pyramid signifies Strength and Duration: The Eye over it & the Motto allude to the many signal interpositions of Providence in favour of the American cause."

- Charles Thomson

*　*　*

Providence Favored the American Cause

What do the words of Charles Thomson really mean? What is the American cause and why did the Founding Fathers choose that particular message? The answer is they saw God do miraculous things for them and felt obligated to acknowledge that this new country came from Him. When you read accounts of the Revolution, many events are described as providential.

On August 27, 1776, George Washington's army suffered a crushing defeat at the hands of a superior British force in the Battle of Brooklyn. Outnumbered more than three to one, Washington's army was now trapped between the British and the East River. Despite the presence of British warships nearby, Washington, on August 29, left with no other option, decided to evacuate the entire army totaling some nine thousand men and artillery across the river. Dangerous currents prevented them from leaving, until around 11 P.M. when the wind died down and the water became calmer. They began the evacuation, small boats traveling back and forth, with General Miflin's brigade left near the lines so that the British would not suspect anything. However, by the end of the night, many, including Washington, had not yet crossed. Benjamin Tallmadge, present during the evacuation, describes in his memoirs what happened:

"As the dawn of the next day approached . . . those of us who remained in the trenches became anxious for our own safety, and when the dawn appeared, there were several regiments still on duty. At this time a very dense fog began to rise, and it seemed to settle in a peculiar manner over both encampments. I recollect this peculiar providential occurrence perfectly well; and so very dense was the atmosphere that I could scarcely discern a man at six yards' distance.

"[Even after the sun rose], the fog remained as thick as ever. Finally, the second order arrived for the regiment to retire, and we very joyfully bid those trenches a long adieu."[4]

Another example is found in an archived edition of the *National Tribune* from December 1, 1880. On the first page, the paper reprinted an interview from the Fourth of July 1859 that Wesley Bradshaw did with Anthony Sherman, an officer under George Washington at Valley Forge in the winter of 1777. He described, using similar language to that of the Great Seal, George Washington as someone who "used often to pray in secret for aid and comfort from God, the interposition of whose Divine Providence brought us safely through the dark days of tribulation."

Sherman, then ninety-nine years old, gives a very detailed account of a pale General Washington who, after leaving his quarters, described to him a mysterious vision. Having given strict orders not to be disturbed, Washington was shocked to see a "singularly beautiful female" standing in front of him. He inquired several times as to her purpose there, but to no avail. Then, trying to continue, a paralysis came over him. The room became cloudy and before him appeared the entire North American continent. The visitor became "airy" in appearance and pointing at the scene said, "Son of the Republic, look and learn." According to Sherman, three times she pointed to war on our shores, each time repeating the words "Son of the Republic, look and learn." The last conflict was the worst of all with the countries of Europe, Asia, and Africa uniting against us. With America on the brink of defeat, she shows an angel above the fray and a white light shines down on the continent, the Americans become energized and win, and the armies of Europe, Asia, and Africa go back across the ocean. Her final words before disappearing were: "Let every child of the Republic learn to live for his God, his land, and the Union."[5]

The founders believed their success came from their allegiance to the Creator. Will America's future be far more treacherous than the past without the same allegiance to Him?

Is it possible that a decline in American Exceptionalism is the result of abandoning the faith of our fathers? What exceptionalism can there be without the Creator of exceptionalism? That is the essence of the Great Seal.

Consider again the words of Thomson: "The pyramid signifies strength and duration. The Eye over it and the motto *Annuit coeptis* alludes to the many signal interpositions of Providence in favor of the American cause." While I am sure he felt a nation should follow Christian principles and that God favored our cause for individual liberty, Mr. Thomson, by using the word *interpositions*, is chronicling an event. He clearly suggests that God actively entered the conflict to create a free society. A free society frees the human potential that He also created. That is American Exceptionalism. It is only common sense that their unanimous approval that day, after six years of unsuccessful attempts while at the same time fighting a war, proved that the seal presented by Thomson expressed their thoughts and experiences. John D. MacArthur describes the task:

"On July 4, 1776, the same day America's thirteen separate states united to declare themselves an independent nation, the Continental Congress took the next step necessary to demonstrate this independence. They began to create their national emblem—the Great Seal of the United States.

During the next six years of the Revolution, three different committees submitted ideas for this graphic image of America, but none were acceptable. On June 13, 1782, Congress turned the task over to their trusted Secretary, Charles Thomson.

Using symbolic elements from all three committees, plus imagery and mottoes of his own, Thomson created a bold and elegant design. A week later, he presented the written description of this two-sided design to Congress, and Congress approved it that same day. The Great Seal of the United States was officially adopted on June 20, 1782."[6]

This emblem's message is supported by numerous speeches, such as that given by Patrick Henry, who also paralleled their war with Great Britain and the Exodus. He said in April 1775:

" . . . that God who had hardened Pharaoh's heart, that he might show his power and glory in the redemption of his chosen people, for similar purposes had permitted the flagrant outrages which had occurred throughout the continent. It was for them now to determine if they were worthy of divine interference, whether they would accept the high boon now held out to them by Heaven; that, if they would, though it might lead them through a sea of blood, they were to remember that the same God whose power divided the Red Sea for the deliverance of Israel still reigned in all his glory, unchanged and unchangeable, was still the enemy of the oppressor and the friend of the oppressed, that he would cover them by a pillar of cloud by day, and guide them through the night by a pillar of fire."[7]

The freedom they fought for attaches a duty to each individual citizen to the Creator. They were serious about what their victory and freedom required of them as seen in these words by George Washington:

"I am sure there never was a people who had more reason to acknowledge a Divine interposition in their affairs than those of the United States; and I should be pained to believe that they have forgotten that agency which was so often manifested during our Revolution—or that they failed to consider the omnipotence of that God who is alone able to protect them."[8] In a letter to Gen. Thomas Nelson, he adds:

"He must be worse than an infidel that lacks faith, and more than wicked that has not gratitude enough to acknowledge his obligations."[9]

Today, the country that fashioned the Great Seal is moving rapidly toward secularism, losing sight of those powerful interpositions the founders felt obligated to acknowledge. Most of us take for granted the motto, "In God We Trust," seen on our currency. Yet, why was it put there? If freedom of religion was guaranteed first, wasn't it because religion was intended to be front and center in American life?

If we are becoming a secular nation, then the Seal becomes hypocritical unless we remove the eye of Providence that we see on it. We create a new seal, with an intact pyramid representing Man at the top again. The end result of that is affirmed by history. If God is not defining morality, truth, and law, then man is . . . and the person that rises up is ultimately the most powerful, and, as history bears out, usually unwilling to share that power. Tyranny, then, can be likened to Godlessness.

However, the outcome is in fact worse. The founders had never seen a time in human history when Man did not acknowledge a power greater than himself. Whether it was the Egyptians, the Romans, the ancient Greeks, or the monarchies of Europe, they all believed in a higher power. It was not until the twentieth century that Man made himself god. Socialism, Communism, Fascism, and Hitler's National Socialism produced the bloodiest century in human history. If America continues on this path, its fate will eventually look the same—only this time she will not be there to rescue herself.

What is America founded on? The original colonies, relying on their faith in God, founded America on the principle of individual liberty, but it is a principle known by them because of their Christian faith. It's important not to judge every aspect of their lives, but instead focus on the gift of our liberty. Unfortunately, because of the overwhelming prevalence of Christianity in the thirteen colonies, it (Christianity) is not mentioned specifically. But it was, nevertheless, seen as the heart of our nation. In fact, in a book that went out of print in 1866, Benjamin Franklin reportedly said:

> **"Had his [Thomas Jefferson's]wishes been consulted, the symbol borne on the national seal would have contained our public profession of Christianity as a nation."** [10]

Rather than a public profession of Christianity, America is closer to a public denial of Christianity.

3

THE SUPREME SACRIFICE

"Greater love has no man than this, that a man lay down his life for his friends."

— John 15:13

IT WAS THE NIGHT OF ENGINE 79 AND LADDER 37'S ANNUAL FIREHOUSE CHRISTMAS PARTY, which has always been held in our quarters. We always remarked about what the night had in store for us because, like clockwork each year, we would go to a rip-roaring fire the night of the Christmas party. I was on duty after this particular party and, like always, after everyone had gone, we cleaned up the firehouse and enjoyed talking about the party, joking about whoever played Santa while waiting for the next emergency call.

In the early morning hours, we heard the dispatcher announce over the voice alarm that a second alarm had been transmitted in the adjoining battalion and, within a few minutes, Ladder 37, or as we say it, "37truck," was called to relocate to another firehouse to replace the company that was at the fire. We in the engine company relaxed, laughing because it was usually the other way around, the ladder company sitting back and watching us leave. Our laughter was short-lived, however, because the voice alarm went off again and we, too, were relocated.

Just enjoying the ride, I put my head back and closed my eyes. It was a pretty long trip and we all knew the way . . . which is why we were surprised when the engine turned down an unfamiliar block. The captain, from the front seat, had thought he had seen smoke, and directed the engine chauffeur to turn. We were shocked because right there, in the middle of the peaceful quiet of the night as we turned the corner, we saw a house fully engulfed in flames. No one outside, no one at their window, and no report of fire until our captain radioed to dispatch, "10-75," the code for a working fire. Unlike the normal call for a fire where the dispatcher might send three engines and two trucks, we knew we would be operating alone for whatever amount of time it would take the other companies to arrive. There was no time to waste. Since it was unreported and because of the time of night, there was a good chance the occupants were asleep inside.

Three of us and the captain advanced the hoseline down a long hot hallway, putting out fire rolling like waves along the ceiling above our heads until we got to the seat of the fire, which had started in the back of the house in a room on the right. There we were met by high heat and dense smoke— smoke and flames were all we could see. As we turned into the room, we knocked down the fire that had overwhelmed that room and began to move in. That is when Mike, who was behind me on the hoseline, urgently called to us. A bad situation was developing. The fire was in a wrap-around hallway and the force of the water stream was pushing it back down the other side of the house, where it was wrapping around and getting behind us, cutting us off from the door. We knew we needed to move fast for a quick "knock-down," rather than completely extinguishing each room. Then, when we knew that was done, we circled back to completely extinguish each room. By this time, Ladder 37 had arrived and began ventilating windows throughout the house searching for victims. We had put out the bulk of this fire by ourselves, and we were finally relieved by the chief now on the scene. We went out to the street feeling pretty good about ourselves and watched the other companies finish up.

That's when everything went horribly wrong. There had been a modest snowfall a day or two before. Tom, who was the roofman that night in Ladder 37, carefully moved to the peak roof along its ridge to ventilate the attic that was still on fire. A peak roof is a dangerous place to be, and he would not normally go there except for extreme life hazard. The battalion had reported firefighters encountering punishing conditions, high heat, and smoke in the attic, asking for someone to help ventilate to facilitate a search and extinguishment. Hearing the urgent call of the battalion chief, Tom, turning around to fully take out another window, briefly put both feet on one side of the roof, only for them to slip out from under him. I remember watching in horror as he slid down the roof, but there was nothing we could do. As if he were in slow motion, he slid down the roof finally going over the edge and down thirty feet to a concrete walk on the side of the house.

Tom was in critical condition, his hip and pelvis shattered, and our firehouse maintained a vigil, someone staying with him in the hospital 24/7 to make sure he had company and that his needs and those of his family were met. Without hesitating, he put himself in a perilous place because he knew it was his duty. He heard the distress of his brother firefighters and was compelled to help. That is heroism on display.

Heroic acts are not a function of IQ or education. They are instead a function of love. Heroism, a byproduct of love, is the willingness to endure personal hardship and take personal risk for the sake of another—and for the firefighter at work, that person is generally a stranger. While the firefighter might not describe his work as a function of love, it is an act of sacrificial love nonetheless and is the reason why an appreciative city erected a memorial in Manhattan to the firefighter.

"To the men of the Fire Department of the City of New York who died at the call of duty, soldiers in a war that never ends."[1]

The late Archbishop Fulton Sheen, famous for his television show, *Life is Worth Living,* gave a lecture at Kansas State University on the word *love.* His point was how, in the twentieth century, the meaning of *love* has become distorted. The reason: while other languages have several words describing all the different emotions attached to what we call love, English uses only the one word to describe them all. "Love, therefore, does not carry any great depths of meaning."[2]

In Greek, the words *eros, philia,* and *agape* are used to identify the different emotions for which we have just the one word, *love.* It is *agape* that describes the sacrificial action that is inseparable from American Exceptionalism . . . or any exceptionalism, for that matter. That's because a shared sense of duty to each other creates a team that can overcome hurdles and obstacles that would otherwise be impossible. Agape represents love that requires nothing in return.

"Now, what kind of love is agape? Love is, in agape, something that is unreciprocated; is loving when love is not returned. It's loving people not because of their functions or their color or anything else, but loving them simply because they are persons."[3]

Division stifles that sense of duty to each other and therefore naturally thwarts our efforts and diminishes our exceptionalism.

"Every kingdom divided against itself is laid waste, and no city or house divided against itself will stand." (Matthew 12:25)

American history is not exceptional because this love was demonstrated by every citizen but because it was woven into American life, our government, the rule of law, etc. Judeo-Christian tradition, the basis for the American system, acts as the watchdog of both government and the rule of law, and is the basis for everything we would call 'American Exceptionalism.' My experiences while serving in the New York City Fire Department provided many examples of self-sacrifice. Amongst us, there are exceptional firefighters who distinguish themselves by their actions above and beyond the call of duty. They produce not just exceptional results, but an exceptional example. They are a model that raises the bar for everyone else.

Teamwork in the fire department can be viewed as a demonstration of the 'American Way,' where duty and sacrifice naturally combine—many roles united for a common goal. On 9/11, examples of duty and sacrifice were done out of love everywhere—American Exceptionalism on display.

But now we are a house divided as new challenges emerge on every front. Historically, America's internal and external challenges were conquered not by an exceptional leader as in the rest of the world, but by a nation that was exceptional by design. As we look at the words of the founders it will become obvious that they felt privileged to be free and called to serve.

Today America must embrace the ideas responsible for her exceptionalism, born of "the laws of nature and of nature's

God."[4] Our leader is not a person, a king, an emperor, or even a president. Nor are we led by a group of people. Instead, America is led by a set of truths. They are the glue that has always united America because they humbly remind us we are equal in value. The Declaration of Independence identified, or better, *codified* every person's dignity and placed a singular duty on government to defend it.

On September 11, 2001, I sat in a Bronx firehouse as a lieutenant and watched the morning news report that a plane had hit the World Trade Center. As it became obvious we had been attacked, I listened to busy radio traffic, the result of two five-alarm responses (one for each tower) that had battle-hardened men anxiously describing a horrifying scene, a constant line of people jumping from the heights of the World Trade Center.

After the first collapse, the Manhattan dispatcher, accustomed to working under stress, nervously called for one unit after another hoping for a report at the scene, instead listening to nothing but complete silence on the other end. Radio traffic had eerily ceased with the dispatcher finally making an urgent plea to any unit on the scene to respond—with no answer. Knowing an aggressive interior attack is standard operating procedure, I fought tears because I knew hundreds of fire-fighters had just perished before my eyes. In the days and months that followed, attending funeral after funeral after funeral, the emotion began to change from sadness to hate. I had replaced the concept of justice with the need for vengeance, a real hatred that was the product of the terrorist's hatred.

Thankfully, in my bitterness, I continued in anguished prayer. I began to feel uneasy, feeling that my reaction and my faith had become disconnected. I shared my anger with God, yelling at times, pointing at the funerals and the wrecked homes, asking why. At the funerals, something besides the obvious grief captured my attention over and over. I stared at the Cross in each church, thought of the suffering it represented, and started to make a connection. Jesus accepted suffering for the sake of all mankind. He didn't refuse suffering because he was the Son of God, he embraced it. My reaction, on the other hand, had been hate-filled vengeance. I wasn't interested in justice. I wanted violence. I thus looked much like the terrorists, not the idealists of our founding. The terrorists had spread their hatred to me like an infection and that's when I began to connect the real long-lasting spiritual harm done to me by the attacks. That is why justice is critical, so that people aren't needlessly left desperate. Seeking justice does not depend on hate, but instead that evil be punished.

In the same way the hero's deed encourages heroism and sacrifice, the hateful deed encourages hate, effectively altering the pursuit of justice with blind retaliation. Justice heals society by recognizing the cost of offenses and demanding retribution. The terrorists continue to succeed as long as we allow hate to replace sober justice because their goal was to change our lives. The hate they produced cannot end with vengeance but instead with real justice, which gives closure to the tragedy. I witnessed many friends who, like me, had embraced the same hate. It made them angry, drained their joy in life, and for some, ruined their relationships.

Today, many years later, the anxiety I saw in myself and my friends after 9/11 is what I see all over America, and it points to a deeper problem. America has always successfully faced dangerous threats and challenges because we were united by one common cause—individual liberty. Our founding documents, by guaranteeing freedom and equality, welcome all people creating the American melting pot. The national debate should include what it means to be a melting pot. Does it really mean celebrating our differences as we have seen lately, or does it mean acknowledging our sameness? Shared liberty encourages a sense of brotherhood and unity that, in America, is understood to be endowed by the Creator.

"He said to them, "Go ye into the whole world, and preach the Gospel to every creature." (Mark 16:15)

Our most famous early American patriots left ample testimony to, and public prayer acknowledging, God's providence. If God was instrumental in the creation of America, and if His purpose was to demonstrate what Man can achieve with Him, then doesn't it follow that future exceptionalism will also be tied to our submission to God? President George Washington, in his first inaugural address, reflected on America's obligation to God, describing an overwhelming compulsion to laud Him.

". . . No people can be bound to acknowledge and adore the invisible hand, which conducts the affairs of men more than the people of the United States. Every step, by which they have advanced to the character of an independent nation, seems to have been distinguished by some token of providential agency. . . . These reflections . . . have forced themselves too strongly on my mind to be suppressed."[5]

Unfortunately, current-day America is moving quickly to secularism. By suppressing spirituality, secularism feeds self-centeredness rather than self-sacrifice because each person becomes the center of all he or she does. Americans have always shared one common goal, to defend and secure individual freedom, and many have sacrificed their lives in the process.

Faith compels a person to consider his or her actions in light of God's commands. The term "American Exceptionalism" that we are so familiar with today did not just pop out of

George Washington praying. (Illustration by Frank Moore, inspired by the memorial at Federal Hall in New York City.)

thin air. It was something that was witnessed and experienced which, finally, was given a label. And one of the most prominent features of that exceptionalism, a feature remembered every Memorial Day and seen from the first day the Pilgrims landed on our shores to today, is the supreme sacrifice made "to secure the blessings of liberty to ourselves and our posterity."[6] American Exceptionalism is neither a work ethic nor a philosophy, nor is it because of any particular genius. Instead, American Exceptionalism is the result of the obedient collaboration of the first Americans with their Creator and the cooperation of Americans since to preserve true freedom. It is appropriate to define American Exceptionalism as God magnifying anything man alone is capable of. The Founding Fathers, recipients of this help, were continuing in the Christian footsteps of their Pilgrim ancestors.

"In the name of God, Amen. We whose names are underwritten . . . undertaken, for the glory of God, and advancement of the Christian faith . . . a voyage to plant the first colony on the northern part of Virginia.. . . ."[7]

Often, firefighters witness horrific scenes and tragedies, many times the result of indifference or malice, that make their efforts seem futile. Yet, while I have met some with a hard and callous perspective on life, I have more often seen a unique, earthy outlook that recognizes firefighters' stand between the innocent and danger. Serving each other brings an inner peace and encourages us to persevere. This is what connects American Exceptionalism to America, the Christian nation.

"And the king answering, shall say to them: 'Amen I say to you, as long as you did it to one of these my least brethren, you did it to me.' " (Matthew 25:40)

Seeing misery firsthand, rather than desensitizing the emergency worker, actually elicits empathy. Every time a firefighter intervenes in a potential tragedy, he nourishes his sense of compassion and his call to charity. He is eager to get into the fray so that he has a sense of purpose. Because of that, many firefighters perished on 9/11 responding to the World Trade Center disaster, despite already being relieved (replaced). Firefighters have always done that, and I am sure it will be that way as long as there are fire departments.

If the hero raises the bar for our own behavior, then Christ serves as the ultimate model for serving our neighbor, making the supreme sacrifice by dying on the Cross. The question is: "What are the consequences of abandoning that model?" Comparing the early success of our nation with the stagnation America faces today can be likened to a science project, taking two petri dishes with the same ingredients and applying different catalysts to them to see how they change. Judeo-Christian tradition, present in the beginning, is being replaced by secularism. Just as in the lab where one compound is different from the other, the old country is different from the new one. Christianity's influence is everywhere in our first century and a half; it is evident in speeches from generals, politicians, and judges, and its presence is the basis for our laws and customs. Yet, most importantly, the essence of Christianity is obvious in our Declaration of Independence, where it connects our freedom to the divine purpose of Man.

A nation without religion has no need of religious freedom. And if the common good, modeled by the life of Christ, is the impetus for the supreme sacrifice, what will come from secularization except a more self-centered society? The Declaration of Independence, by saying we are "endowed by our Creator," means we are indebted to God.

"That the Deity is a being of great goodness, appears in his giving life to so many creatures, each of which acknowledges it a benefit by their unwillingness to leave it."[8] (Benjamin Franklin)

How can anyone rationalize giving up his own life except by recognizing something greater than one's own life? Christ's Cross is the ultimate model for the supreme sacrifice which assures us of a better life to come.

Innovation and technology have made people self-reliant and without the discipline of Christianity, we can be tempted to become our own little islands, growing indifferent to our neighbor. Compassion, just like the muscles of the body, must be exercised or else it atrophies. The aftermath of the 9/11 attacks exposed an ailing American culture that had lost self-respect because the purpose of life is not correctly understood without Christ's example. If we do not see our personal duty as one of charity, we will give that duty to confiscatory government, empowering it in a way that was not intended. As limitations on government erode, so does individual liberty.

*   *   *

In February 1987, I began my career as an NYC firefighter at the Fire Academy at Randall's Island in Manhattan. During the first week or so, guest speakers and documentary accounts of firefighting tragedies intermixed with physical training and firefighting lessons hammered home to us the real risks associated with our new careers. One of our speakers was a disabled firefighter whose left side of his face had been disfigured at a building fire in Manhattan. His message, in a nutshell, was that firefighting was the greatest career in the world and he had no regrets. These guest speakers were provided to make clear the dangers of the job, and a few people did in fact leave. Most of us, however, felt it an honor to be there and that we now would actually make a difference in people's lives. I believe that this kind of optimism—knowing that you can make a difference—can change the course we are on as a nation. Our efforts are encouraged by the outward-looking lens provided by Christianity that teaches us to love our neighbor.

Later that week, we "probies" were shown a particularly shocking documentary film about the fire aboard the aircraft carrier *USS Forrestal* in 1967. After a rocket was accidentally fired from one of the aircraft on the flight deck, it hit another plane, igniting a severe fire. The firefighters went to work immediately but were instantly killed as Korean War-era bombs from other planes exploded. Tragically, these team members were the only ones onboard trained for firefighting, and the well-intentioned sailors who replaced them made matters worse. The film showed sailors trying desperately to read directions on masks and equipment that they had never been trained to use as the fire spread to the living quarters below deck. Our fire academy trainers wanted the anxiety and confusion shown in that scene to be a lesson on preparedness they were trying to instill in us.

That documentary taught many lessons, among them the duty we have to look out for each other. What would have happened if no one else had been willing to accept the risks? On my first day of training at the Fire Academy at Randall's Island underneath the RFK Bridge, I read a sign that said, "Let no man's ghost come back to say, 'My training let me down.' " Based on my career and experience, I would add that nothing great is achieved without self-sacrifice. Self-sacrifice extends beyond firefighting to our responsibility as citizens. The recipe for American Exceptionalism is the same recipe for all countries—Christian charity and sacrificial love.

That first summer, after a few months of seeing nothing but small fires, I was anxious to show what I could do in a serious fire—and I finally got my chance. Afterward, I learned that the career I thought of as an adventure was actually a matter of life and death for the people who counted on the firefighter. It was early in the morning when we pulled up to a two-family house in the Bronx with heavy fire conditions on the first floor. I jumped off the truck and began running toward the house, setting into motion a comedy of errors. First, a fireman from another company slapped me on the shoulder and said, "You forgot your helmet." I was mortified, and by the time I had gone back and retrieved it, my lieutenant was already inside the house and nowhere to be seen, at least not by me. The Battalion Chief, seeing my probationary patch and identifying company number, pointed me upstairs. Trying to recover some dignity, I donned my mask and, trying to make up lost time, bolted up the stairs into blinding smoke. I couldn't see. Hearing noises to my right, hoping to quickly rejoin members of my company, I forgot to maintain contact with a wall and crawled straight through the black smoke until I collided with a table. I continued stumbling my way along, never finding my lieutenant. Finally, thinking my best move would be to go back and start at the beginning, I turned and crawled to where I thought the stairs should be. Instead, I was now traveling in circles. I became frustrated and yelled several times, "Where are the stairs? Where are the stairs?" Just then, someone tapped me on the shoulder. I looked up and saw the engine company lieutenant standing there, hunched over looking at me, no mask on[9], and grinning. He calmly pointed to the right to the smoke-hidden stairs about eight feet away. Confident now that I was not alone, and trying to look composed, I thanked him while pretending to know where I was. I proceeded in the opposite direction to search the house and find my company . . . and I lost that staircase again! Only this time, I would not look for help and luckily, after the fire was knocked down, the air finally cleared up enough for me to find everyone. That was the disappointing beginning of my firefighting career. Although quite humbled, my consolation prize was the confidence I gained from seeing a team at work, confident in each other and what they could do.

"We must, indeed, all hang together, or most assuredly we shall all hang separately."[10] (Benjamin Franklin)

Getting our country back on track is more than just being unified. Loving our neighbor, and empathizing with them heightens our efforts. A nation is not exceptional because of the efforts of one man—it is because of the efforts of many, working together. Each man's charity strengthens the bonds of unity throughout society. These bonds are not forged merely by coming together for serious shared causes. They are also built by living life together, sharing good times and bad. The more we can make ourselves part of each other's lives, the closer we all become and the more we are able to work together. These are the things that make life more enjoyable and what I was blessed with as a firefighter. The firehouse was the small-scale version of that community.

Firefighters seem to know this instinctively and reinforce those bonds, often by practical jokes that get everyone involved. I remember one night, Chuck, a senior man (senior in rank), went up to his bunk early and someone heard him snoring. We all took the opportunity to tie a rope around the leg of his bunk in the dark and stretch it to the pole hole on the other side of the room. We dropped it down to the apparatus floor below, and then we went downstairs. Everyone took hold of the rope and, on the count of three, ran, pulling the rope as fast as we could. We could hear the bunk sliding across the twenty-five feet to the pole hole and Chuck screaming like a little kid, until the leg of the bunk fell into the hole. The screaming stopped, replaced by the rumble of feet. Chuck, a big man, ran downstairs in a fury, but our hysterical laughing as he chased us finally got the best of him and he stopped, cursed a little, and then a smile came over his face. Practical jokes are one tool often used to build the camaraderie necessary for the dangerous situations we will face. Hopefully, we learn to laugh at ourselves and take ourselves less seriously. In the firehouse, the self-centered guy would soon be left alone . . . and he eventually knew why. It is simply *selfishness* versus *selflessness*. Selflessness encourages unity, which is an irreplaceable source of a country's strength! We must rediscover our neighbor and show him compassion if we are to reunite our country. Our country's exceptionalism produced so many exceptional institutions like the FDNY. That is why the officers union uses as its motto, "In unity there is strength."[11]

* * *

The Battle for Peace
God forbid we should ever be twenty years without such a rebellion.. . . . The tree of liberty must be refreshed from time to time, with the blood of patriots and tyrants.[12]
—Thomas Jefferson

I remember reading the preceding quote by Jefferson for the first time and trying to make sense of it, naively thinking how could Jefferson have looked at times of peace and not consider them more desirable than times of war? But after my experience on 9/11, as I witnessed firsthand the devastation around Ground Zero, this quote suddenly came back to me. This rebellion against the government found sympathy from Jefferson, who was part of the government. In the same letter, Jefferson said:

"Can history produce an instance of rebellion so honorably conducted? I say nothing of its motives. They were founded in ignorance, not wickedness."[13]

It is obvious from this statement that, to Jefferson, the government and the citizens were united, motivated by the same vision for their country. The colonies were struggling to realize the dream of the sovereign citizen, and both were committed to that vision. The convictions of Jefferson the President were the same as his fellow Americans, which demonstrates a unity in early America that disregarded social status. However, the more important point demonstrated here is the other battle that he recognized. His America was very different from the America we are familiar with. In his time, spiritual speech was not separate from political speech. They were merged, not merely for effect, but rather because they saw the natural marriage of faith and reason. This becomes more and more obvious as one explores the writings of the founders.

For Jefferson, the blood of patriots and tyrants is equivalent to the perpetual war between good and evil. The absence of this eternal struggle is impossible because evil is never absent. It appears in the tendency toward sin that we all struggle with. The degrees of apathy and fear determine the advance of evil. How do we gauge this war between good and evil in a secular culture? Today, every battle is considered an affront to peace, so the ongoing battle necessary to defend liberty, the battle between good and evil, is missed.

"To avert war or chastisements, nations must return to God and have a rebirth of the spirit of prayer.. . . This atmosphere of prayer must be revived in our country, not that we might get something but that we might become something; not that we might sugarcoat our living with a veneer of piety, but that we might abandon our natural selfish way of thinking and living and put on the mind and spirit of Christ."[14] (Fulton Sheen)

Throughout Scripture, God has responded favorably when man has acknowledged Him as Lord. To forgo the battle against evil is nothing less than surrender that allows Satan to trample upon what is good. The early colonies in the North, such as Plymouth, began as places for people to freely serve God. It is the reason our ancestors traveled to America. Thus, Jefferson and his contemporaries naturally identified the tyranny of King George with the perpetual struggle with evil. This freedom and their relationship with God were interconnected.

"*To avert war or chastise-ments, nations must return to God and have a rebirth of the spirit of prayer.... This atmosphere of prayer must be revived in our country.*"
- Fulton Sheen

"All experience hath shewn that mankind are more disposed to suffer, while evils are sufferable, than to right themselves by abolishing the forms to which they are accustomed. But when a long train of abuses and usurpations, pursuing invariably the same object evinces a design to reduce them under absolute Despotism, it is their right, it is their duty, to throw off such Government, and to provide new Guards for their future security."[15]

The peace that we should seek is not the absence of conflict. It is, instead, the tireless quest for true justice.

Jefferson's assertion that the tree of liberty must be refreshed from time to time, with the blood of patriots and tyrants, simply acknowledges good must stand against evil. Today we fight physical battles, just as in the past . . . with one exception . . . we are ignoring the spiritual war. The more that the gospel is made irrelevant in the public square, the more evil will manifest itself. The peace that we should seek is not the absence of conflict. It is, instead, the tireless quest for true justice.

"The best definition of Peace the world has ever had is that given by Saint Augustine: 'Peace is the tranquility of order.' It is not tranquility alone . . . Peace adds to quietude the idea of 'order' . . . Since peace is order it follows that peace is inseparable from justice . . . Peace is the work of justice indirectly insofar as justice removes the obstacles to peace.. . . "[16] (Fulton Sheen)

4

THE CROSSROADS

S PIRITUAL BATTLES DISTURB THE WORLD'S PEACE IN A DIFFER-
ENT, more profound way than physical conflicts do. That's
because spiritual battles divide people on the basis of opinion
as opposed to physical threats that tend to unite those threatened by a common enemy. Many current campaigns targeting
social justice and discrimination issues have this effect, all
while much of America accelerates its shift to secularism. In
this shift, the truths that once brought people together are
being redefined; that's especially (and most importantly) the
case with freedom, which is no longer grounded in personal
duty but is more often defined by what is owed to you. The
deep concept of God-given rights secured by a government
that derives its "just powers from the consent of the governed"[1] is being replaced with a materialism that confuses
rights with entitlement.

"If the state is the source of rights, then the state can dis-
possess man of his rights. In other words, the principle of democracy is the value of the human person, which owes its
origin to God. It owes it also to Christ, the Son of God, who
preached to us the worth of a single man, against whom He

balanced the entire material universe in his question: 'What doth it profit a man if he gain the whole world and lose his soul?' "[2] (Fulton Sheen)

The 1960s ushered in a new president whose inaugural address reminds us of the timeless principles on which this nation was originally founded and, at the time, was still committed. That address by John F. Kennedy defined America no differently than Washington, Adams, or Jefferson had. With Communism actively opposing us via the Cold War, America was easily distinguished from the oppression of the Soviet Union. American Exceptionalism doesn't rely on majority holiness of any generation of Americans, but it does depend on faithfulness to her origins and faithfulness to the Creator. President Kennedy's words, spoken almost two centuries after our independence, remind us of our obligations and duties as free people.

> We observe today not a victory of party but a celebration of freedom symbolizing an end as well as a beginning signifying renewal as well as change. For I have sworn before you and Almighty God the same solemn oath our forebears prescribed nearly a century and three quarters ago.

> The world is very different now. For man holds in his mortal hands the power to abolish all forms of human poverty and all forms of human life. And yet the same revolutionary beliefs for which our forebears fought are still at issue around the globe—the belief that the rights of man come not from the generosity of the state but from the hand of God.

> We dare not forget today that we are the heirs of that first revolution. Let the word go forth from this time

and place, to friend and foe alike, that the torch has been passed to a new generation of Americans born in this century, tempered by war, disciplined by a hard and bitter peace, proud of our ancient heritage, and unwilling to witness or permit the slow undoing of those human rights to which this Nation has always been committed and to which we are committed today at home and around the world.

Let every nation know, whether it wishes us well or ill, that we shall pay any price, bear any burden, meet any hardship, support any friend, oppose any foe, in order to assure the survival and the success of liberty . . . "[3] (Inaugural address of President John F. Kennedy, January 20, 1961)

President Kennedy was assassinated November 22, 1963, along with many of the principles he stated. A rapid escalation of the Vietnam War was met by protests that were more opposition than debate among Americans. The government began to be seen as a separate entity from the American people. The sexual revolution, defended as a rejection of old authority, was nothing more than a surrender of self-discipline. The temptation of self-gratification, addicting by nature, became the public debate rather than public shame. The 1960s can be seen as a crossroads pointing to a new path where contraception and abortion paved the way for marital infidelity, damage to family life, loss of human dignity, and lost respect for human life. This new path continues to lead America away from what made her exceptional: God and His truth. This path no longer sees our prosperity as something that God has given. Even though we recognize our stumbling, we continue on this path; in fact, we choose to quicken the pace. The two paths

travel in opposite directions: the old path toward exceptionalism and the new one toward stagnation.

Freedom and prosperity become their own pitfall if they
are not accompanied by self-discipline. Struggle forces people
to reflect on their weakness, and it is humbling. Prosperity,
on the other hand, leads to complacency and must be accompanied by temperance; otherwise, our abundance points us
toward gluttony, pride, and sloth. The Gospel of Jesus is a natural defense against this complacency because it reminds us
of our obligation to serve God and neighbor. Prosperity then
becomes a tool to better serve. As Jesus said,

"Enter by the narrow gate; for the gate is wide and the
way is easy, that leads to destruction, and those who enter by
it are many." (Matthew 7:13)

On September 11, 2001, evil gave us a convincing push
for which we no longer had the muscle to resist. Most will say
that we've been fighting the enemy and shedding our blood
since 9/11, but we are missing a deadlier enemy. The American
way is the culture of freedom that is protected by the Declaration of Independence. We are ruled not by men but by nature's
God. It is not just America, but also the American way that is
under attack—not just physically by terrorists, but also spiritually by an anti-God malevolence. This evil attacks from
within while we look outside for enemies, oblivious to the real
problem. The Christian principles that are the foundation of
America and, in fact, Christianity itself are under attack by
people around the globe, including Americans, both Christian
and non-Christian. The definition of marriage, the sanctity of
human life, and questions of gender identity are the most obvious assaults on absolute truth, but virtually every previously
held truth is in question, including our freedom itself as we
see in media censorship or the banning of certain speakers.

Freedom depends on the rule of law, but what does the rule of law depend on? Law cannot be rudderless, and it is not. The rule has a ruler acknowledged in the Declaration and He is not man. The prodigal nation must turn back to God for freedom to remain for our children.

How does a society oppose evil? How do its citizens recognize the enemy before it is too late? In the late nineteenth and early twentieth century, America and the world witnessed evil in the form of the Armenian genocide. As a God-fearing nation, we were obligated to defend humanity. Yet, while Presidents Chester Arthur, Grover Cleveland, and William McKinley all expressed outrage over the brutality of the Ottoman Turks, their words did nothing to stop the evil. Theodore Roosevelt identified the problem. The perpetual war between good and evil demands God-fearing people fight for what is right. He said:

"Armenians, who for some centuries have sedulously avoided militarism and war, and practically applied advanced pacifist principles . . . are so suffering precisely and exactly because they have been pacifists . . .

"Wrongdoing will only be stopped by men who are brave as well as just, who put honor above safety, who are true to a lofty ideal of duty, who prepare in advance to make their strength effective, and who shrink from no hazard, not even the final hazard of war, if necessary, in order to serve the great cause of righteousness."[4]

The battle between good and evil must always be visible wherever evil is found, but it takes God to receive the wisdom needed to recognize the evil—and the courage to fight it. Our humble beginnings are marked by a revolution that epitomized this battle of good and evil.

"These are instances of, I would say, an astonishing Providence in our favor; so that we may truly say that it is not our arm that has saved us. The hand of Heaven appears to have led us on to be, perhaps, humble instruments and means in the great providential dispensation which is completing."[5]
— **Samuel Adams**

* * *

America . . . in Name Only
"There is little value in insuring the survival of our nation if our traditions do not survive with it!"[6]
— **John F. Kennedy**

The original *Superman* TV series of the 1950s described Superman as "faster than a speeding bullet, more powerful than a locomotive, able to leap tall buildings in a single bound," eventually finishing with "fighting in a never-ending battle for truth, justice, and the American Way." In a bygone era, Americans naturally understood what that meant, and, in fact, that is why that phrase is part of the opening monologue. Allegorically, Superman represents America. The opening of the show is effective, not because it is a radical assumption, but instead because the association between truth, justice, and the American Way are accepted by the audience and the words capture the spirit of American Exceptionalism, a can-do attitude that recognizes the fight. The TV show's opening recognizes the aforementioned perpetual fight between good and evil.

America is not just a place, nor is it a race of people. While other countries can trace their origins to a particular ethnicity or race, today's America began with a creed that elevated every person's self-worth to equality with all, great or small. The truth that God created us equal, the truth that is the underpinning of our government, has a natural attraction to mankind. That truth eventually overwhelmed an entrenched society that had justified slavery. Frenchman Alexis de Tocqueville came here in the 1830s and wrote *Democracy in America* because the world was aware something extraordinary was happening here. The world was witnessing the upheaval of the ageless societal division between the people and government. Uprooted, it was replaced with a government of, by, and for the people, rooted in Christian thought and profiting from unleashed potential.

"The American Revolution broke out, and the doctrine of the sovereignty of the people came out of the townships and took possession of the state. Every class was enlisted in its cause; battles were fought and victories obtained for it; it became the law of laws."[7] (Alexis de Tocqueville)

In America, the idea of sovereignty of the people emanates from God, not man, when we state as a nation that God created us equal and endowed us with inalienable incontrovertible rights. And, an America "under God," as stated in the Pledge of Allegiance, also has the ability to clearly see her enemies because they challenge what God has given Man, specifically, his liberty. However, what happens if we eliminate the common understanding of God we started with? Most people see Western society as under attack but see this attack as simply a physical threat to our national security, such as when media reports show ISIS brutally executing someone. Such reporting generates questions about how to prevent it in the future, without grasping the deeper question of why the threat exists in the first place.

Today, America is ignoring a more nefarious enemy, far more dangerous than the evil aims of ISIS. This is a spiritual enemy that attacks her virtue. Judeo-Christian thought that uniquely defends individual liberty is under attack, not by foreign governments but instead from within. So-called progressives in America have embraced Communist philosophies from the last century, denigrating and distorting our founding documents, especially the First Amendment. Cries of "hate speech" make our freedom of speech subservient to how people feel about our speech. Laws coercing churches to compromise their beliefs are destroying those churches' ability to properly shape public morality. Thus, in a very rigid hateful fashion, no different than our enemies, we are paving the path of destruction of our freedoms. Americans, by extracting God from the public square, are extracting the root of American Exceptionalism.

"... all men are ... endowed by their Creator with certain unalienable rights ... "

America's Declaration of Independence forcefully reminds the world that America has a divine purpose to defend the rights of the common man from tyrannical ideologies. But that defense is also needed here.

"There is little value in opposing the threat of a closed society by imitating its arbitrary restrictions ... There is little value in insuring the survival of our nation if our traditions do not survive with it."[8] (President John F. Kennedy)

God gives us exceptionalism in two ways: physically through His blessings to our land and spiritually in the strength and resolve that come from faith in Him. President Kennedy gave a frightening warning in that speech in 1961, and his words are proving to be prophetic. Every time I see people attacked for what they believe, as is happening on college campuses all across the country, I see us looking less like one nation under God and more and more like the enemies we oppose. Sadly, in my recognizing this, I see national repentance as the only way God will give America the grace to recognize and the courage to repel the enemies of liberty. They need to be seen before they can be fought.

How can we propose to fight evil when we no longer care about being good? I, after operating at Ground Zero, confused justice with judgment, and the result looked more like hatred. Opposing our enemies by imitating them, as Kennedy pointed out, is what we must never do. It is wisdom that pursues peace, not by ignoring conflict but by opposing evil in all its forms. Even parents addressing their child's anger quickly learn that the best results are seen not when punishment is dispensed angrily or rashly, nor by ignoring the child, but when well-discerned discipline is calmly and fully meted out. That is how true justice works.

* * *

The "9/11" Infection

"But I say to you, love your enemies and pray for those who persecute you, so that you may be sons of your Father who is in heaven; for he causes his sun to rise on the evil and the good, and sends rain on the righteous and the unrighteous."
— Matthew 5:44–45

I witnessed something remarkable at Ground Zero after the World Trade Center collapsed—not just the outpouring of generosity and appreciation for my fellow firefighters, which was beyond belief, but a unified effort from everyone who happened to be there to contribute whatever and however they could. There were people of such diverse backgrounds, as only can be seen in New York City, all working as one. I think it was a pretty good demonstration of what is great about our melting pot and what fosters American Exceptionalism, namely Christian charity and sacrificial love, a recipe every nation can pursue.

Today, the value of our diverse cultural "melting pot," touted as one of our greatest assets, is being confused with diversity for its own sake. Rather than the beauty of cultures uniting as Americans, in appreciation of our founding beliefs, the focus is placed on our differences. The word "American" is hardly seen without a hyphen in front of it and the list of 'hyphenated' groups seems to grow every day. Diverse cultures united for the American way give us strength, but if diversity is lauded apart from what makes us the same, diversity encourages division. On 9/11, America identified a particular ethnic group that attacked us because they hated us, but that hate has spilled over to us. It is a 9/11 infection that the terrorists brought which is changing our society. It is an uneasiness that causes cynicism toward those we don't know and throws tolerance out the window.

This was the most successful terrorist attack on American soil, not because of how many people the terrorists killed, but because of the permanent effect it had on our country. The greatest threat to America is not the threat of physical harm to our citizens, but the erosion of our freedom and our commitment to the founding principles that defend it. Elected representatives have stoked the 'fear' of the people instead of being a sign of strength and hope. The creation of the Department of Homeland Security and the passing of the Patriot Act have given the government access to our privacy without weighing the potential damage to the protections guaranteed in the Bill of Rights. Security suddenly leapfrogged over freedom on 9/11, a train that must be turned around for the sake of our posterity.

This is more than the terrorists could ever have hoped for, but worse, fear is also an essential step toward despotism. The highly charged emotions of fear and hate impair reason. Further, responding to hate with hate, people begin to cease to consider justice and the will of God. The danger becomes replacing respect for life with revenge. Protecting human dignity becomes the priority if we believe in God and see human beings as part of God's design. It is what is protected by our founding. This is what has always attracted the 'tired masses' of the world and also why America will always be targeted by evil and the liar, Satan. "The fear of the Lord is the beginning of wisdom." (Proverbs 1:7)

In the days following 9/11, a relative suggested to me that we should just nuke Afghanistan . . . or better yet the whole Middle East. This 'kneejerk' reaction is without forethought. The prevailing terrorism threat must be dealt with like any threat, with wisdom . . . but where does that wisdom come from? Wisdom itself is not acquired. No one takes a course on how to be wise. Rather, it is a gift that comes when we love our fellow man as God does. It is enhanced by knowledge, a knowledge that starts with loving our Creator.

"Love justice, you that are judges of the earth . . . For wisdom will not enter into a malicious soul nor dwell in a body subject to sins." (Wisdom 1: 1–7)

In this battle between good and evil, the terrorist is limited physically . . . but not spiritually! It is no different than the martyr who is prepared to die for the faith. The former is willing to die for evil, the latter for good. Without a courageous response for justice from leadership, citizens begin to retreat, and the result is a systematic enslaving of herself in the name of security. From freedom comes a great wealth of courage. But a courageous response gains no traction without courageous leadership. From the first moments after the World Trade Center was attacked, first responders and New Yorkers, not politicians, heroically worked to restore order and relieve suffering in downtown Manhattan. A political answer to the threat of this enemy has been to give security a higher priority than liberty, resulting in a more dangerous threat: the citizen's freedom being sacrificed to defeat terrorism.

"They who can give up essential liberty to obtain a little temporary safety deserve neither liberty nor safety."
-Benjamin Franklin

Our own ancestors won for us freedom, knowing that the free society was not the safe society. Benjamin Franklin sums up their thought:

"They who can give up essential liberty to obtain a little temporary safety deserve neither liberty nor safety."[9]

We are in solidarity with every generation of Americans who have defended their freedom. It is an extraordinary and moving fact that the Holy Bible proclaims "Do not fear" 365 times. On September 11, 2001, my own faith was shaken, and it was not until I reflected on what had been taught to me about life that I made sense of the suffering. When people have everything they want, when they fear no daily danger, they no longer seek any help, especially that of Almighty God. If a people's confidence is shattered and they don't know where to turn for help, there is panic.

By missing the current spiritual danger, we intensify the current physical danger. Society needs to relentlessly oppose evil. While God is love, He does not tell us to ignore evil. The challenge for America is to recognize evil, seek justice, and leave judgment to God. But that's not possible if we do not want a relationship with Him.

Freedom depends on justice because freedom must co-exist with evil and would be defenseless without justice . . . but that is not the same as judgment. Judgment implies knowing why someone acted. "Judge not, that you be not judged. For with the judgment you pronounce you will be judged and the measure you give will be the measure you get." (Matthew 7:1–2). On the other hand, justice is an action. It is defined by Webster's dictionary as "the administration of law based on what is just; that is, what is deserved, merited, and fair." If American justice depends on her laws, then those laws must be fair to be just, but how is that determined except by unchanging, unwavering, absolute standards? Man's law depends on God's law because it is unchangeable and the resulting justice heals an injured society. America, to be exceptional, must have that same effective justice that she had in the past, real justice that comes from the truth preserved by Christianity.

Modern American culture, preferring scientific and technological advancement, is busy chipping away at Judeo-Christian values that are needed to heal discord and encourage unity among people. Without them, the infection the 9/11 terrorists brought with them runs unimpeded. The Gospel supports unity naturally by encouraging individuals to correct themselves rather than others. This is not, however, our natural impulse; as we move away from our Christian roots, we move toward hate and revenge.

This consuming emotion of 'an eye for an eye' becomes habitual, just as it does for the terrorist. Evil generated a hateful attack on America that infected us when we began to hate the attacker, and now habitual hate is being aimed at each other. Americans are battling one another over issues of race, gender, religion, income, and politics—just about anything. Yet the true cause of these internal wars is secularism polluting our ideals. Therefore, before we do anything else, America must show remorse to God before she can restore exceptionalism. Can we? Can our nation wear the proverbial "sackcloth and ashes" in repentance and restore God's favor?

Hatred needs to be replaced with charity, exchanging one for the other. America is about looking out for the downtrodden, the afflicted, and the persecuted. Tragedy, trials, and affliction can build character in people if and when endured . . . or reduce weak-minded people to a state of dependency. The difference depends on whether we succumb to fear or have faith. Saint Peter, walking on the water, became frightened and began to sink.

"Peter got out of the boat, and walked on the water and came toward Jesus. But seeing the wind, he became frightened, and beginning to sink, he cried out, 'Lord, save me!' Immediately Jesus stretched out his hand and took hold of him, and said to him, 'You of little faith, why did you doubt?' " (Matthew 14:29–31).

For us to receive His helping hand, we will need to appeal to Him. We need to pray as a nation for our faith to be restored and then have faith that he will come to our aid.

Over the years since the World Trade Center collapse, I have personally spoken to a number of firefighters who now deny the existence of God because of 9/11. They asked, "How could God allow such suffering!" One of the hardest things for anyone to do is to see beyond their own personal grief; at least it was for me. But looking at suffering from a different angle may help and may even give us strength. If we remember Christ is the Son of God, we can change the question to "How could Christ allow such suffering?" God then doesn't just see our suffering, He shares in it because Christ is suffering. That is proven by His Cross. The founders understood true religion to have its roots in Judeo-Christian tradition. Had they said, "All men are endowed by Christ with certain inalienable rights" rather than "the Creator," the Declaration would have more accurately represented their beliefs.

Suffering is truly personal and can point us to God's love if we remember Christ's suffering. While there is certainly a threshold for suffering, nothing of value is ever achieved without at least some suffering. A priest recently told me, "It's not suffering that's bad; it's sin that's bad." And he is right! We all can name times when people have encouraged each other through times of terrible suffering—suffering that might have been unbearable without such encouragement. Every army that has marched into battle has experienced it. And for Christians, the greatest encouragement is the Cross which reminds us that God is not oblivious to our pain; He, too, endured it. We are an exceptional nation because we are a Christian nation with the Cross as a backdrop to encourage us through adversity. Today, it seems our national tolerance for suffering has greatly diminished. Is it the result of making our Christian roots obscure and insignificant?

"Could God have justified himself before Human history, so full of suffering, without placing Christ's Cross at the center of that history? . . . He is not the Absolute that remains outside the world, indifferent to human suffering. He is Emmanuel, God-with-us; a God who shares man's lot and participates in his destiny . . . The crucified Christ is proof of God's solidarity with man in his suffering. His omnipotence is manifested precisely in the fact that He freely accepted suffering. He could have chosen not to do so . . . If the agony on the Cross had not happened, the Truth that God is Love would be unfounded."[10] (Pope John Paul II)

That truth is hard to accept when suffering strikes us personally. This is why we need community. This is one of the most important components of charity—to lift each other up in times of tragedy. This is how our fellow man finds the love of God when he is unable to find it on his own.

Returning to prayer was the remedy for the "9/11" infection for me because it caused me to reflect on my beliefs, especially on eternal life. If America is to continue to be successful, she must first recognize her reliance on God who loves us and trust Him. Together with God, America will tackle her threats with wisdom and certainty.

Love is best understood as charity. The principle of charity becomes strength the more we citizens collectively practice it. Conversely, hate is weakness because we act in fear, isolating and dividing ourselves. Today we are becoming so divided that it is hard to see a light at the end of the tunnel—but it is there. "One nation under God" is indivisible. If America acts in awe of God, He will continue to bless us. On September 11, 2001, we were given a great reminder in the midst of the horror. As the towers collapsed, two pieces of steel fell, distinguished from the rest of the burning rubble, and formed the sign of the Cross. God was not pulling any punches. The appearance of this cross wasn't to remove the rubble, it didn't return our friends, and its purpose was not to end suffering on earth. Instead, it reminded us then, and should continue to remind us, that God is always present and that He does not abandon us but instead shares our suffering! The 9/11 Cross should remind us of the life that awaits us.

Cross naturally formed in the debris at Ground Zero in New York City following the 9/11 attacks in 2001. (Photo by Anne M. [Bybee] Williams, reprinted with permission.)

5
THE HERO'S CROSS

"I shall need the favor of that Being in whose hands we are, who led our fathers, as Israel of old, from their native land and planted them in a country flowing with all the necessaries and comforts of life; who has covered our infancy with His providence, and our riper years with His wisdom and power..."[1]
— **Thomas Jefferson, in his first message as president**

CHRIST, IN THE SACRIFICE OF HIS LIFE, GIVES MANKIND THE PERFECT DEMONSTRATION OF HEROISM. He placed every human being ahead of himself and, in so doing, He gives value to suffering. Conversely, the secular movement in America indulges the desires of the people supplanting God's authority with Man's. Without imposed boundaries, the will of the people creates a cultural egoism that slowly moves 'self' above everything; it ignores the example of sacrificial love and true heroism that Christ represents. Ultimately, secularism must be repulsed by Christ because He is the opposite of secularism. Today, personal accomplishment is being confused with true heroism and Man pridefully sees himself as sufficient. Eventually, without God at the top, the strongest and loudest voice will again lead. America must remember God gave her freedom or risk replacing King George III with a twenty-first century version.

"We cannot ignore God in our national life and expect Him to be with us in our international relations. We cannot revolt against God in our consciences and expect peace in our country."[2] (Fulton Sheen)

We are a creation, entitled by Nature's God with certain unalienable rights. "That to secure these rights, Governments are instituted among Men . . . "[3] From the Christian perspective, if rights come from God, then Satan, the enemy of God, is the enemy of our rights. He finds evil men to corrupt our rights, and we must pray that God provide heroes to fight for them.

* * *

Exceptionalism from the Ashes
"Where there is no knowledge of the soul, there is no good . . . "
— **Proverbs 19:2**

The morning of 9/11, on my way to the Division 6 office, I was thinking about what the fire companies needed to do at the Twin Towers, putting myself in the shoes of the responding firefighters. I had been advised by the house watchman of the plane crash, but I didn't yet realize the gravity of the situation. Knowing there was a television upstairs, I hustled up to the office to see what was happening.

I met a deputy chief, reporting for his first tour in Division 6. He hurriedly asked me to help his aide get everything together because he was sure he would be relocated to

Manhattan. As I was doing that, I looked up at the television tuned in to live coverage of the World Trade Center. I was watching the intense fire in one of the towers, when, suddenly, from the side of the screen, we could see another plane coming out of nowhere and crashing into the other tower. I was trying to make sense of it; at first, I thought I must be seeing a replay, but it was obvious that it was live coverage. I called to the chief who was now almost out the door, "Chief, something is going on here. You better come take a look and see what you're going to; I think another plane has hit the towers."

Not completely hearing me, he said, "I haven't got time," and he continued out the door. After the first collapse, the department radio was silent for several minutes. The silence wasn't broken until I heard the chief's voice from his car en route on the FDR Drive. He broke the silence by saying, "Division 6 to Manhattan. Division 6 is on the FDR about fifteen minutes from the World Trade Center, K."

The next day, in the early morning hours of the twelfth, a team of five firefighters from Engine 71 and I were able to join the search and rescue operations on "the pile," the name given to the World Trade Center, now a pile of rubble. For a long time, we just stood at the command post, watching small bits of debris falling like snow all around us, waiting for orders until, finally, several hours later, we were called to work. Eventually making our way around the perimeter of the disaster, I saw the chief I had met the day before at quarters, nearly thirty hours earlier. After some twenty hours extinguishing random fires and searching in vain, we were finally relieved . . . by that same chief, still on duty after all this time. It was almost four days before he finally returned to the quarters of Division 6.

As the search was being conducted on 'the pile,' a very dangerous fire was raging throughout the seriously damaged

Marriott Hotel, a fire exacerbated by an inability for fire-fighters to use the surrounding fire hydrants. Another of our deputy chiefs who was off duty came to division head-quarters after hearing of the attacks. He took his gear and immediately went to the World Trade Center and took command of the operations at the Marriott. The FDNY overcame the structural instability of the hotel, fire on multiple floors, a shortage of equipment, and no available water, and it extinguished the massive fire over a period of several days. But he stayed at the scene the entire time, commanding the efforts while ensuring fire companies were relieved and replaced with fresh companies.

I mention these two deputy chiefs because of the unusual stamina and perseverance they exhibited working under those conditions for days without rest. They are examples of conduct above and beyond the call of duty that encourages others to fight on when they might otherwise be inclined to quit. I met firefighters who had been retired for many years, now old, who came to the division headquarters, found spare gear, and went down to the site. All of New York City's first responders, as well as emergency workers from all over America, construction workers, and private citizens all joined together. Their examples of courage and fortitude inspired the country. Heroism is unique in its ability to inspire the efforts of all who see it.

"For if you love those who love you, what reward have you? Do not even the tax collectors do the same?" (Matthew 5:46)

*   *   *

M.I.A.

One man's courage can inspire others to exceptionalism . . . provided he can be seen of course. So, what are we looking for in a hero? Will he look like Iron Man or Mother Teresa? Real heroism has nothing to do with appearances but everything to do with actions. Firefighters are seen as heroes because there is public perception of the dangers associated with firefighting. Yet Mother Teresa demonstrated great selflessness in her own unique way, forgoing any semblance of normalcy or comfort in her life, placing herself in great physical danger, all to serve the suffering and dying. And, more incredibly, she did this for her entire life.

Most acts of heroism are born in the moment. Each act is unique and exceptional. However, to expect the hero of one day to be continuously exceptional is unrealistic. There is no perfect superhero. Common people do exceptional good, too, and yet, they, just as all of us, are also guaranteed to fail in the future. That is human nature. American culture today is quick to scrutinize the hero for flaws. For example, the retired neurosurgeon, Dr. Ben Carson, in his run for the Republican nomination, suddenly became a "liar" rather than an exceptional surgeon when his account of an offer to attend West Point was labeled inaccurate. Because of the permanent damage scandal does to one's reputation, every accusation must be researched and verified before going public. That last step appears to have been thrown away.

Most of us can think of similar examples of individuals who, if not for some exposé, would otherwise be a model for the rest of us. Even though our military and police do heroic work every day, their reputations suffer when stories about individual soldiers and officers concerning improper conduct or worse become front-page news. During political campaigns, opposition research digs up stories of impropriety that the general public gladly consumes. Countless books are written that dig in to previously unknown aspects of the private lives of renowned Americans that usually malign their reputations. Of course, real criminal behavior must be dealt with, but it is important to weigh potential harm caused by stories that do not need to be told. Achievements need to be seen in our culture because they create enthusiasm.

Courageous Americans aren't disappearing. Instead, they are being obscured, missing in action so to speak. Our modern secular culture seems motivated to discount heroism. Why? Is it because the culture has become immature and self-conscious, afraid greatness will shine a negative light on their behavior? It is often painful to examine your own life, to analyze your own failures and fears. Achievers show us our own mediocrity, and it takes maturity to admit their greatness. That is why some may find it comforting to point out faults in them.

" . . . that the light has come into the world, and men loved darkness rather than the light, because their deeds were evil. For everyone that does evil hates the light, and does not come to the light, lest his deeds should be exposed." (John 3: 19-20)

The two chiefs I mentioned inspired me to endure more and to sacrifice more. Inspiration comes first from watching the hero in action, and then it continues as long as we remember those heroes . . . or until some scandal is revealed concerning their private life. Then the good deed is all but forgotten. Any time we see a public figure being accused, we should be slow to judge and ask, "Is justice the goal or is there some malicious objective being sought?" Today there are petitions to remove monuments to Columbus, Washington,

Jefferson, Lee, and others. If successful, ask yourself what will be gained and what will be lost? Modern progressives are challenging our early beliefs such as the free market, our Christian roots, and even the Constitution itself; and we should cherish the debate. But let's not merely cause one side to disappear by discrediting them. America should be afraid of sacrificing her history for a politically correct agenda mostly because that history has been one of incredible and unimaginable success. By failing to acknowledge real heroes, we do not merely lose sight of their deeds; we lose the example and the inspiration for our own exceptionalism.

If our country is not setting higher goals, then what are we settling for? Exceptionalism might as well be replaced with mediocrity. Heroism breeds heroism, and defeatism breeds defeatism because people naturally follow the example of others, especially when confronted by adversity. What they see will either encourage or discourage them. This is why Americans need to avoid envy and the temptation to tear down achievers. The less we acknowledge courage, the less courage we will see in everyday life.

*   *   *

The Challenge

There is an old expression, "You can't see the forest for the trees." It means that you shouldn't get lost in minute detail while ignoring the big picture. Addressing our problems starts with an underlying philosophy, an overall viewpoint from which you govern your actions. That is followed by an honest analysis of the things that need to be fixed, always keeping your eyes on that big picture—"the forest." In America, the erosion of our national identity is resulting in a general anger and anxiety that I can feel in public. The country that self-identified as a Christian nation is being forcibly changed, and what we were will be lost if we don't do an about-face.

Our identity has always been clear. We are the only nation in history that was built upon the intentions of our Creator for our individual liberty. This makes us exceptional, and it is from this American spirit that true heroes are born. The heroic war between Good and Evil on the world stage is always played out as a war between freedom and tyranny. And in America, heroes from all walks of life have emerged to fight that war because Christianity sustains true heroism. It does this by specifically coming to the defense of our individual liberty. Most of the world's population can be divided into five major religions: Judaism, Christianity, Hinduism, Islam, and Buddhism. Yet, out of all of them, Christianity alone defends our innate freedom as individuals. This makes Christianity essential to the American philosophy that identifies "liberty" as an "unalienable" right.[4] The hero's purpose and reason for sacrifice is identified by this unmistakable connection between Christianity and America.

The very first pages of the Bible give us the defining statement of Judeo-Christian tradition when God declares that we are made in His own "image" and "likeness." (Genesis 1:26–27)[5] In that sense, Judaism and Christianity share the same ideological defense of human freedom, that the better we know God, the better we know ourselves; and the first thing we know about God, implied just a few pages earlier, is that He is free. It says, "In the beginning God created heaven and earth." (Genesis 1:1) God is not coerced or obliged by any force or person to create, He is not told to do so, and He has no compelling need to create the earth. He does so by His own Will. He is a person just as we are persons.

To further emphasize the point, we learn later that God warns Adam, "you may freely eat of every tree of the garden; but of the tree of the knowledge of good and evil you shall not eat . . . " (Genesis 2:16–17)

Of course, tragically, Adam and Eve eat the forbidden fruit despite the warning; they were obviously free to do so. God doesn't smack their hands, saying, "Hey dummies, I thought I told you not to touch that." He does not stop them because He created them free.

The Gospels later give a deeper spiritual meaning to human freedom that we can apply to religion. In several accounts of miraculous healings, Jesus charges those healed to tell no one what He did for them. For example, in the Gospel of Matthew, two blind men are healed by Jesus when He "touched their eyes." He then tells them, "See that no one knows of it." (Matthew 9:29–30) Again, in Mark, Jesus healed a man who is deaf and dumb by touching his ears and tongue, crying out "be opened." But Jesus then "charged them to tell no one." (Mark 7:32–36) He is not trying to gain followers through miracles. He is not coercing anyone to follow Him. Instead, Christ's objective is that you follow Him for no other reason than because you love what you hear. Coercion, on the other hand, means someone is pressured to act and is the antithesis of free choice. Thus, exposure to the life of Christ and Christian doctrine teach respect for human freedom. Recognizing that helps us understand the Founding Fathers' devotion to not just their own liberty, but the liberty of Mankind, and helps us share their zealous defense of liberty. Heroism and exceptionalism, therefore, are cultivated by freedom and Christianity.

Some may ask, "You're telling me I have to be Christian. What about freedom of religion?" In reality, it is quite the opposite. Christians have been commanded to be amongst non-Christians. And He said to them, "Go into all the world and preach the gospel to the whole creation." (Mark 16:15) This is not a command to 'preach to the choir' but instead to welcome non-Christians. So, we, as a Christian nation, defend freedom of religion precisely because our Gospel objects to coercion, presuming non-Christians will freely bring their personal beliefs and compare them to the Gospels. It is unique in its concern to give truth to all people. True conversion is seen as a gift, and never trumps a person's freedom. For these reasons, complete religious freedom in America actually depends on our Christian form of government for its defense.

The other world religions neither come to the defense of individual liberty nor promote exceptionalism. India, which is about 97 percent Hindu, developed a caste system, and it would be ridiculous to think they would develop a system contrary to their own beliefs. How can the caste system possibly promote freedom or exceptionalism? If Albert Einstein and William Shakespeare were born into the lowest caste, what would they produce? You would probably see Einstein cleaning toilets or Shakespeare digging ditches. Neither would get the chance to achieve his full potential. There would be both the obvious assault on their liberty and a road block to their exceptionalism. Here, our guaranteed pursuit of happiness, at least in theory, would allow these men to be exceptional. Under the caste system, exceptionalism becomes accidental, a matter of chance because Einstein and Shakespeare would have to be born into an upper caste to succeed. Regardless of whether everybody achieves their full potential, America, as a Christian system of government, pushes the needle toward exceptionalism while Hinduism and the caste system push the needle away.

The other world religions similarly hinder exceptionalism and individual liberty in theory and practice. Islamic societies that place women and infidels in a position of inferiority have effectively placed half of their society at a disadvantage, thus limiting both their freedom and their potential achievements. Buddhism does not stress an essential reality. It does not believe in the soul and sees the individual ego as a delusion. "A person is in a process of continuous change, and there is no fixed underlying entity."[6] Naturally, a diminished conception of your unique individuality does not give the same respect for or need to defend individual freedom. Without the focus being on the individual, individual rights have diminished importance.

America is a Christian nation because of her founding documents and not because of how many Christians there are. However, it will take Christians to push back the aggressive secular culture, rediscover the source of her convictions, and return us to the path that made us exceptional. In the process, new heroes will emerge motivated by those that came before them.

*　　*　　*

Setting the Bar

How can there be a great civilization without any expression of heroism? A great nation becomes great precisely because it has produced great people. To answer why heroism is a natural byproduct of a great society, you must first correctly identify what motivates a hero! In my experience, that motivation comes from seeing someone in need. I have called heroism the "high bar" of achievement because it sets a standard and models exceptional behavior that inspires others. Most people never consciously aim for that high bar; instead they find that fate has placed them in a position they never anticipated, and they respond as a hero unconsciously because they feel a duty and responsibility to do so. It does not enter their mind to leave it for someone else to do.

In the emergency services, whether the average citizen actually sees an individual firefighter or police officer actually do something heroic is secondary to what we know from past experience about firefighting and policing. Their example is one of perseverance that reminds me of the sacrifice of those who came before us. Their example forces us to confront our own purpose in society, a purpose that is now measured by service.

While it is true that America faces a great challenge today, the purpose of this book is not simply to sound the alarm. It is to recognize how the concept of freedom and the model of heroism have both been distorted. No great society has ever emerged without its people answering a unified call to sacrifice for that society. But the maturity of the Christian society, where all are called to take up their cross, calls every citizen to individual personalized acts of heroism whose fruits are shared by the entire society.

Baseball Hall of Famer Rod Carew was once at a benefit for doctors seeking a cure for childhood cancer, when he asked all the doctors in the room to rise. Carew then spoke:

"People talk about us as heroes . . . baseball players, football players, hockey players . . . ladies and gentlemen, these (doctors) are heroes. They're the ones that change the lives of so many of us, and they will continue to do so because they care."[7]

While many of us get it, I fear many Americans have become numb to the exaltation of public figures at the expense of those Americans who truly change lives.

If we do not recognize or do not *want* to recognize America's real heroes, then what would that say about us? An exceptional nation must know her heroes, especially if it hopes to duplicate that heroism in the future. Acts of heroism do not come easy; there is always a price attached to it, a personal sacrifice. But for liberty to survive, everyone should be willing to sacrifice to the best of their ability. Freedom will be challenged, sometimes from the outside . . . and sometimes from within. And, those internal attacks require courageous opposition as much or more than external ones.

Whom then do we emulate? Rod Carew gave us the answer. "They're the ones that change the lives of so many of us . . . because they care." To label achievement as heroism is to merely link it with personal accomplishment. There are a couple of inescapable ingredients for an act of heroism. First, it must be sacrificial. Second, it should respond to a critical need. A Tom Brady touchdown pass with one second remaining to win the game might be exciting to watch, an example of exceptional skill and self-control, but we should never call it heroic. Affixing that false label glorifies a gift that, in and of itself, does nothing for society and, in the process, cheapens the title we save for those who risk and even give their lives for others. It also obscures the small acts of heroism people do for each other every day.

Heroic acts are found in every walk of life, at every income level. Heroism is displayed in various forms and in varying degrees. Over the course of American history, heroes have been put on display as a source of inspiration and to set the bar high. Collectively, they show what can be accomplished if we have the will. That is precisely why it is imperative that we cherish our heroes' past and identify them in the present. Because if future achievement is encouraged by the high bar set by those true heroes who came before, then it is negatively impacted when we set the bar so low that we all can simply skip over it. For what is achievement?

> " . . . while we are using the means in our power, let us humbly commit our righteous cause to the great Lord of the universe, who loveth righteousness and hateth iniquity. And having secured the approbation of our hearts by a faithful and unwearied discharge of our duty to our country, let us joyfully leave our concerns in the hands of him who raiseth up and putteth down the empires and kingdoms of the earth as he pleaseth . . . "[8] (John Hancock)

Why must we achieve? Among the animals of God's great creation, we are the only ones with vision, and the achievement of our vision often takes heroic efforts. By answering one question, we answer why we need heroes. Here in America we have a rich heritage of heroism that originates with the Pilgrims. They came to this continent not knowing what lay ahead, and they endured incredible hardship. From the exploration of the New World to the exploration of the West, from the Revolutionary War to World War II, we have applauded the actions of our own ancient heroes in thanks for their sacrifice and for teaching us what is truly worth fighting for.

Looking beyond our American history, there are examples of heroes in biblical times. Whether it is Abraham called to sacrifice his son Isaac, or David going where no soldier would go in slaying Goliath, their actions encourage every generation to act bravely when their own instincts would beg otherwise. The understanding of heroism was changed, perfected, and clarified by the life of Jesus Christ. The words of Jesus command everyone to take up his cross and follow Him, in effect commanding everyone to be heroic. America and its meteoric rise on the world stage can arguably be attributed to a nation filled with unsung heroes inspired by Christian teaching.

Contrast that era to today. Our society confuses achievement with heroism, adding Lebron James and Bruce Springsteen to lists containing George Washington and Audie Murphy. A society, able to recognize and acknowledge true heroes, thrives because it feeds its compatriots with examples of sacrifice and the societal message of what is worth fighting for, e.g., God, family, country, and freedom itself. It requires all of us to enter that fight for what is true, good, and right, relying on God all the while to reveal those things to us and give us the spirit to fight. Exceptional heroism requires a recognition of things more important than one's self; selfish motives limit heroism because the cost of the act is given importance. Thus, we can exclude feats done for glory's sake. Christ, to accomplish his mission, knew He had to experience death. He provides the ultimate model of heroism. It is human nature to seek the easiest path, but history proves that real freedom has only been possible through heroic efforts taken to oppose the oppressor. If Christ is the model, we cannot choose as rights that which Christ himself would oppose.

I was in a car recently with three West Point cadets. Two of them engaged me in a lively debate concerning the hot social topics of the day—the third one remained silent. At the end of the trip, the first two cadets left the car, while the third lingered. I said, "Did you lose something?" He answered, "No sir, I want to talk more about those social issues. I think of myself more as a fiscal conservative and a social liberal. It seems like the only way to get things done. What do you think?" He probably already knew what I believed. I said, "You don't have to go far to find that train of thought. Most people would say the same thing." In our country, why would someone feel uncomfortable expressing their own values? Why should someone feel that they must become a social liberal to get things done? I asked him to think about something. "Maybe it is precisely our stance on the social issues that determines all our other decisions." He pondered the idea, as we expanded on what makes us American—our freedom.

Today, it takes valor to defend our Judeo-Christian tradition in the face of vehement opposition from influential, well-funded groups—opposition that sees courage and heroism as enemies to progressive utopian goals. In fact, I believe what we learn from the life of Christ is the support of heroism. As our founders said in the very infancy of our nation:

"And for the support of this Declaration, with a firm reliance on the protection of Divine Providence, we mutually pledge to each other our Lives, our Fortunes, and our sacred Honor."[9]

Displays of heroism in our early years sprang from "a firm reliance on the protection of Divine Providence." Jesus Christ himself points out that the man who hears his words and acts on them is like the man who built his house on a solid foundation so that his house still stood when the torrents came. The man who did not act on those words is like the man who built his house on sand—when the torrents came, the floodwaters washed away his house, and it was destroyed. Is our American house similarly being ruined? We must stand for what is permanent; in America, it is our individual liberty. And this liberty is only fully understood in the context of our being made in the image and likeness of God. Our "solid foundation" is a foundation that is immovable when we believe, and yet it only exists if we believe. We must rediscover the courage to defend the revealed Truth of

Judeo-Christian tradition, and as we do this, we will see clearly who our heroes are.

"Everyone then who hears these words of mine and does them will be like a wise man who built his house upon the rock; and the rain fell, and the floods came, and the winds blew and beat upon that house, but it did not fall, because it had been founded on the rock. And everyone that hears these words of mine and does not do them will be like a foolish man who built his house upon the sand; and the rain fell, and the floods came, and the winds blew and beat against that house, and it fell; and great was the fall of it." (Matthew 7:24-27)

PART II

FIGHTING AMERICAN EXCEPTIONALISM

6

ASSAULT ON HEROES

"Those who pay no regard to religion and sobriety in the persons whom they send to the legislature of any state, will soon pay dearly for their folly. Let a man's zeal, profession, or even principles, as to political measures, be what they will, if he is without personal integrity and private virtue as a man, he is not to be trusted."[1]

— John Witherspoon,
signer of the Declaration of Independence

I N THE ONGOING WAR BETWEEN GOOD AND EVIL, a free country must value and applaud virtue, seeking it always to be prepared for internal threats to freedom. Infamously, Vladimir Lenin is credited with saying, "If you want to make an omelet, you must be willing to break a few eggs." That statement completely devalues the human individual—his ends being all that matter and his (or any despot's) means being automatically justified. In Lenin's Marxist vision, the life of the individual is ancillary to his vision of the whole society.

That terrible illegitimate concept for society is the polar opposite of the American founding premise that all individuals are born equal. In contrast to Lenin, America was formed to protect the "eggs." When authorities serve themselves, they obviously are not "for the people." But the American experiment contradicts this age-old demonstration of power and exploitation. A country where the citizens are the sovereigns, where they have the power to determine how the country is run, will always be challenged by man's lust for power. The men who risked all to create our form of government exhibited the rare virtue of being disinterested in power.

It is important to remember the critical lessons of the twentieth century. This is a desperate time for liberty. The end can only justify the means for the person who believes his ambitions must not compete with or be impeded by anyone else's views. The American Way is citizens as sovereign in life because they are subservient to God in spirit. If the Creator alone is the master, then no man can claim that role. If the ends of those in power are all that matters, then the opposing views of others do not matter.

* * *

United We Stand . . . Divided We Fall

Firefighting requires teamwork to succeed, and teamwork naturally requires you to freely put the team before yourself. When any member of a fire company is unable to complete his task, someone else must, so each member feels duty-bound to fulfill his assignment. I remember the story of a fire in a store on Jerome Avenue in the Bronx. There were people trapped in the basement and there was no way to get them up to the main floor because of the inferno burning up there. The captain of the truck company on the scene knew collapse of the main floor was imminent, went to the basement of the adjoining store with his inside team, and breached a brick wall between the two stores. The team made it in time to rescue those who were trapped next door.

Despite the dangers of firefighting, a firefighter's allegiance to his brothers and sisters encourages heroic acts that would not otherwise be chosen. Revolutionary Era Americans made their own personal success secondary to the cause of liberty. They fought alongside their countrymen for their posterity. If they had put their own interests first, they, most likely, would never have taken the risks that they did. The American way is Americans united in the defense of freedom.

"We, therefore, the Representatives of the United States of America, in General Congress, assembled, appealing to the Supreme Judge of the world for the rectitude of our intentions, do, in the Name, and by Authority of the good people of these Colonies, solemnly publish and declare, That these united Colonies are, and of right ought to be Free and Independent States . . . And for the support of this Declaration, with a firm reliance on the protection of Divine Providence, we mutually pledge to each other our Lives, our Fortunes, and our sacred Honor."[2]

✳ ✳ ✳

The War Against the American Way

"There is nothing more common than to confound the terms of the American Revolution with those of the late American War. The American War is over; but this is far from being the case with the American Revolution. On the contrary, nothing but the first act of the drama is closed."[3]

— **Benjamin Rush,**
signer of the Declaration of Independence

The war for your freedom is not so much a physical or even an ideological war as much as it is a spiritual war. The Founding Fathers were well aware of this when they said we are endowed by our Creator with certain unalienable rights. Among these are life, liberty, and the pursuit of happiness. Because the fight for freedom is spiritual, it does not have an end! And that knowledge should make us wary of subtle threats to liberty that might otherwise be missed. If free people take for granted where their freedom comes from, they will leave themselves open to evil.

"At what point then is the approach of danger to be expected? I answer, if it ever reach us, it must spring up amongst us. It cannot come from abroad. If destruction be our lot, we must ourselves be its author and finisher." (Abraham Lincoln)[4]

The American Way of government of, by, and for the people is under a calculated disdainful assault here at home. Democracy is the voice of the people, and America is intended to protect that voice, yet what vehicle today can you trust to hear what the people say? Even social media sources, originally touted for their ability to give everyone a voice, have been caught filtering speech. YouTube and Twitter have had to apologize for removing conservative opinions from their sites.

Those given authority have a duty to encourage the people in difficult times rather than amplify their fears. This unfortunately is what I see America doing to herself post 9/11. The outward enthusiasm that inspired us, as in World War II, to take it to the enemy has been replaced by a somber self-criticism in search of what we might have done wrong to inspire such hate. And worse, those with power in both government and the media pit us against each other. For instance, several years ago the Tea Party emerged as a good example of a grass roots democratic movement, yet it was maligned by members of Congress. When Senator Ted Cruz, a product of the Tea Party, encouraged members of the House of Representatives to defund the Affordable Health Care Act, we saw not intelligent debate but deceitful propaganda. Even though the Tea Party had made that their main platform, Senator Harry Reid labeled Republicans fighting to defund it as "anarchists and extremists,"[5] maligning all opposition to the Affordable Care Act with language originally reserved for terrorists. In light of the current climate in government, Senator Ted Cruz's firm stance is heroic, not because it is right as much as he demonstrates willingness to fight for what he believes and the people he represents, regardless of the abuse.

✳　✳　✳

Freedom of the Press

While the party system is one assailant to the American Way, the second assailant, the information media, is more powerful. Historically, the media, charged with the noble task of informing the people, would investigate candidates, challenge an administration to explain what it was doing, and ask the crucial question of "Why?" Slander was not the norm in journalism.

For the sake of its citizens and the virtuous society, the information media must be committed to hold our elected government accountable to the truth. It is why our original governors, the founders, added the First Amendment which says, "Congress shall make no law . . . abridging the freedom of speech, or of the press, or the right of the people to peaceably assemble, and to petition the Government for a redress of grievances."

While these three freedoms (speech, press, and assembly) are usually topics discussed separately, I believe they are mentioned together here to remind both government and citizens that they are the tools protected by law to ensure that the people can effectively petition the government through the most effective means. These are protections our founders knew had never existed for the citizen; however, the press, critical for the defense of liberty, no longer provide unbiased information we can use to accurately look at the world. Aleksandr Solzhenitsyn, coming from a government that controls the information media, the Soviet Union, told us what he sees as the direction of the American press. This is part of a speech at Harvard in 1978, and it is amazing how much this applies to what we have in the media today, forty years later!

> "The press too, of course, enjoys the widest freedom. (I shall be using the word *press* to include all media.) But what sort of use does it make of this freedom? . . . What sort of responsibility does a journalist have to his readers, or to history? . . . How many hasty, immature, superficial, and misleading judgments are expressed every day, confusing readers, without any verification? The press can both stimulate public opinion and miseducate it . . . Hastiness and superficiality are the psychic disease of the twentieth century and more than anywhere else this disease is reflected in the press . . .
>
> "Enormous freedom exists for the press, but not for the readership because newspapers mostly give enough stress and emphasis to those opinions which do not too openly contradict their own . . . "[6]

We have been on the so-called progressive path for more than fifty years now, a path that is leading us away from exceptionalism. The three safeguards to freedom controlled in repressive regimes, from Cuba in the West to North Korea in the East, must be defended or they will be lost here as well. Ronald Reagan said:

"Freedom is never more than one generation away from extinction. We didn't pass it on to our children in the bloodstream. It must be fought for, protected, and handed on for them to do the same, or one day we will spend our sunset years telling our children and our children's children what it was once like in the United States where men were free."[7]

"The confusion becomes worse because this change of meaning of the words describing political ideals is not a single event but a continuous process, a technique employed consciously or unconsciously to direct the people."
- F. A. Hayek

Carefully chosen, high-charged words that connote either positive or negative reactions are used in media to label people and ideas. They are powerful tools that are being used to sway opinion to a chosen point of view. Rather than providing facts to support informed choices, broadcast and print media are describing events with emotional agenda-driven words for partisan purposes. And it is important to be skeptical when we see it. The Nobel Laureate F. A. Hayek commented on how language can be altered to perpetrate propaganda.

"We have already seen how the same (change of meaning) happens to 'justice' and 'law,' 'right,' and 'equality.' The list could be extended until it includes almost all moral and political terms in general use. If one has not . . . experienced this process, it is difficult to appreciate the magnitude of this change of the meaning of words, the confusion which it causes, and the barriers to any rational discussion which it creates . . . And the confusion becomes worse because this change of meaning of the words describing political ideals is not a single event but a continuous process, a technique employed consciously or unconsciously to direct the people.

Gradually, as this process continues, the whole language becomes despoiled, and the words become empty shells deprived of any definite meaning, as capable of denoting one thing as its opposite and used solely for the emotional associations which still adhere to them."[8]

After September 11, 2001, both government and the media successfully separated the perpetrators of the terrorist attacks from Islam by attaching the words *radical* and *extremist* creating a new term, *radical Islamic extremist.* As Hayek previously illustrated, "emotional associations" were attached to the new term. Today, the words *radical* and *extremist* are attached by Americans to those they oppose politically or ideologically, preferring to denigrate the opposition rather than debate. In these instances, a free press is necessary to soberly separate emotion from information, to give both pros and cons on the particular topic to its audience. Instead, they repeat the disparaging remarks while, at the same time, leaving out many details. This should scare any intelligent person because it is a sabotage of that first purpose of the freedom of the press—to petition the government for a redress of grievances—because it is failing to hold government accountable and failing to give the people information necessary to make good choices.

Courage is displayed any time Americans peaceably assemble to petition the government, and even more so when they continue despite being targeted for doing so. However, without the press reliably delivering the truth, the people's ability to redress the government unravels. In two ways it (the press) inevitably becomes a tool for the powerful; first because the masses will be without reliable information, and, second, because government will have the coercive power to shape what is called "information."

At the heart of the founders' plan of self-government was

the protection of the citizen's ability to be informed and communicate true facts and voice opinion free of coercion and propaganda. However, simply protecting the right of free speech is only half the battle. It is of little help to the free society if people charged with delivering information are not honest and committed to the truth. If people cease to place priorities on sound information, instead communicating only to serve themselves, how long will it be before the press replaces the task of informing with attention grabbing stories? President John F. Kennedy warned of this more than fifty years ago, but that warning was ignored!

"... Our press was protected by the First Amendment—the only business in America specifically protected by the Constitution—not primarily to amuse and entertain, not to emphasize the trivial and the sentimental, not to simply 'give the public what it wants'—but to inform, to arouse, to reflect, to state our dangers and our opportunities, to indicate our crises and our choices, to lead, mold, educate, and sometimes even anger public opinion."[9]

The language of the First Amendment is clear: "Congress shall make no law . . . abridging the freedom of speech, or of the press; or the right of the people peaceably to assemble, and to petition the Government for a redress of grievances." Our government is prevented from limiting the press; this is so that the people can be knowledgeable of what the government is doing—the only way the people can possibly know what needs to be rectified. President Kennedy is simply restating the purpose of the freedom given to the press, and its purpose is critical to our liberty. However, "to lead, mold, educate . . . " is only beneficial if the information being delivered is true.

*   *   *

Does the End Justify the Means?

In the present day, we must be wary of popular 'ends' being used to popularize unconstitutional, and ultimately dangerous 'means' to accomplish those 'ends.' I say dangerous because those extra-constitutional means quickly diminish the constraints put on government to limit its power. One example involves our Second Amendment right to keep and bear arms. For example, tragedies like the Newtown, Connecticut, and Orlando, Florida, massacres are exploited, capitalizing on public shock, to persuade citizens to give up a right that is constitutionally protected—the right to keep and bear arms. Since no one wants to ever see a tragedy like that again, people feel the need to change something and are more easily persuaded, never weighing the potential consequences. It is interesting to note that governments globally are moving to disarm their citizens while the United Nations has crafted a global ban on handguns. The end result will leave weapons solely in the hands of the world's military. That is precisely why this right was important to our founders—to protect future generations from tyranny by giving them a means of physical defense. It distinguishes us from most of the world and creates a shared and personal responsibility for the protection of freedom.

*　　*　　*

American Sweat

"Until comparatively recent times few people seriously confused . . . 'freedom from' obstacles . . . with the individual freedom that any kind of social order can secure. Only since this confusion was deliberately fostered as part of the Socialist argument has it become dangerous."[10]

— F. A. Hayek

The curse of God found in Genesis says, "By the sweat of your face shall you get bread to eat, until you return to the ground from which you were taken . . . " (Genesis 3:19). If you give credence to the Bible, then you see an admonition aimed at you. Implied in the verse: effort equals bread to eat; no effort equals no bread to eat . . . and more effort means more bread to eat. The common temptation, exploited by Communism and Socialism, is comparing what you have to eat to the next person. The message from God in Genesis is a message to you and me, as individuals, to work. But once I begin to look over my shoulder at my neighbor, I eventually fall prey to envy by taking the focus off me and putting blame on another. It is a negative emotion that, rather than calling you to positive change, instills in you some animosity for your neighbor. Christianity asks you to look to those neighbors who suffer, and to show compassion, and not to envy those who succeed. Where the Socialist says every man's industry should produce the same outcomes, God has put the burden of proof on each individual to reap the fruit of his own efforts. And that is the first step toward exceptionalism.

It is senseless to seek to exchange the American Way, with its unmatched success, for something that has proven to fail time and time again. Socialism is a true evil that has left misery in its wake as brutal regimes viciously abuse and expand their power. Remembering the commandment, "Thou shalt not covet thy neighbor's goods," reminds us that this Socialist tendency, to want what your neighbor has, is evil. Before we lose to Socialism, we might learn something again from President Reagan:

"If we lose freedom here, there is no place to escape to. This is the last stand on Earth. And this idea that government is beholding to the people, that it has no other source of power except to sovereign people, is still the newest and most unique idea in all the long history of man's relation to man."[11]

✶   ✶   ✶

He Who Is Without Sin

"It is not the critic who counts; not the man who points out how the strong man stumbles, or where the doer of deeds could have done them better. The credit belongs to the man who is actually in the arena, whose face is marred by dust and sweat and blood; who strives valiantly; who errs, who comes short again and again, because there is no effort without error and shortcoming; but who does actually strive to do the deeds; who knows great enthusiasms, the great devotions; who spends himself in a worthy cause; who at the best knows in the end the triumph of high achievement, and who at the worst, if he fails, at least fails while daring greatly, so that his place shall never be with those cold and timid souls who neither know victory nor defeat."[12]

— Theodore Roosevelt

While the founders gave God credit for our nation, modern America gives him none, instead criticizing our founders. Once our ancestors placed firm reliance on God, they became confident. God won a war with heroes only He could create. Along with the dramatic expansion of media over the past several decades has come a tool by which the most influential heroes are reduced to flawed, average people or, worse, morally corrupt and lustful. John F. Kennedy was declared a hero because of his actions after the sinking of *PT 109*. This display of leadership assisted in his election to the presidency. Yet today, he is identified more by disparaging allegations of extramarital affairs than by his heroic courage in the face of death, a courage whose display is a matter of history that should not be erased. Models of exceptionalism today are similarly disappearing. Christians are taught that we are all sinners in need of forgiveness. That comes with the understanding that there is no perfect person. Why do we relish in reducing those who have been exalted for their achievement?

Searching in another man's closet for flaws undermines American Exceptionalism. Real evil, of which the media are unwitting dupes, seeks to make achievers less admirable by tarnishing their reputations. The America that emerged in 1776 is an obstacle to the ambitions of the powerful. I have seen 9/11 bumper stickers that say, "Never Forget." We must never forget that we were attacked because we represent freedom. We must never forget that freedom will always be opposed by those who thirst for power, and we must never forget that our enemies are those who would usurp our sovereignty.

Unfortunately, it seems that it has become habitual for the media, after recognizing the exceptional accomplishment of someone, to hunt or patiently wait for a story that will tarnish the person's image. The need to find flaws with achievers can be a prideful temptation if it is born out of self-consciousness. I think it would benefit America to do a cultural examination of conscience because I see an immature tendency to view someone's superiority as our own inferiority rather than as a model.

We need the example of exceptional people and cannot afford to destroy it by demanding they succeed in all things. Society is busy having a masquerade party for heroes, glorifying phonies while tossing a blanket over the real thing. It is indicative of a societal immaturity that sees achievement as a threat and is afraid to admit inferiority. The self-conscious may feel that if we tear them down, we no longer feel inferior, we can settle for mediocrity, and most importantly, take the spotlight off of our own weaknesses.

While it is always necessary to be truthful in order to correctly define what is right, we must be careful to resist destroying people's reputation. As Saint Paul used the analogy of the one body having many parts, a nation is made up of individuals, and their talents are divided among the whole people in every form. A person, great in one aspect, should be expected to be flawed in others, and thus, no person can be expected to be a model in every way. It is important not to try to make them so. Yet, with the expansion of media, this is exactly what has happened. Enemies of freedom have every tool they need to reach into our homes, and in us they find a willing audience for their attack on models of excellence.

Pride prevents us from acknowledging our fellow citizen, and I am afraid we have made the conditions in which no model of heroism can survive for long. It is easy to envision any number of news programs proudly revealing some decades-old skeleton in the closet of some patriot. We don't need critics today! They are a dime a dozen. We need Christian soldiers in every arena of life to say no to immorality and yes to virtue. Evil is continually seeping into every aspect of society including religion, and it must be met with stalwart opposition!

7

THE HOME OF THE BRAVE

IREFIGHTERS FEEL THAT MOST OF THE TIME WE ARE JUST
DOING OUR JOBS. We make a point of acknowledging exceptionalism by giving out medals. Yet amongst us, the word *hero* is rarely used. This is a manifestation of the real underlying fact about heroes, namely that they originate, not just in a given person, but are extracted by an event. When President Kennedy, in an interview, was asked regarding his actions on *PT 109*, "How did you become a hero?" He replied, "They sank my boat."

Heroes sometimes are made by events with fate drawing out the hero. Yet, individuals can also force the hand of fate by putting themselves in harm's way for the benefit of others. This is what observers see and admire in the firefighting vocation that also causes them to attach the title of hero. I remember hearing someone arguing that because of the recent reduction of fires, maybe firefighters should take a reduction in pay. A friend of mine answered, "We're not paid for what we do but for what we might have to do." And thank God there are some that, perceiving a societal good, will take on increased risk to ensure that good.

It is necessary to make the distinction here between different types of action. If you contrast the glory seekers, thrill seekers, and risk takers with heroes, the difference boils down to the goal and the reward. For instance, thrill seekers, such as extreme sports athletes, are very obviously into it for the adrenaline rush. Ancient heroes might be categorized as glory seekers looking specifically to receive the accolades that come with victory. But real heroes come from a different place because, ultimately, they see good coming from their actions, a good that depends on the benefits others receive from the risk they've chosen and not from the adrenaline rush or the accolades.

"Far be it from us to do such a thing as to flee from them (the enemy). If our time has come, let us die bravely for our brethren, and leave no cause to question our honor."
—1 Maccabees 9:10

*   *   *

Recognizing Heroes

Take a moment to think about what makes a hero. One afternoon I was working as a lieutenant in the Bronx. My company responded to an alarm, and on arrival we found an apartment on the third floor fully engulfed in flames. I found the front door ajar and was able to proceed a few feet into the apartment, when, suddenly, intense heat drove me to the floor. With me was a probationary firefighter at his first fire. I proceeded through the front room where the heat became so intense that I had to lie on the floor to avoid being burned. It was at that time that I saw the probationary firefighter right behind me. I shimmied further down the hall and found the source of the fire and also found that the "probie" (probationary firefighter) had stayed with me the whole way. We quickly made our way back to bring the nozzle man with the hose line toward the fire. This probie firefighter was at his first fire, a dangerous one where one of my men was burned as he vented the fire escape window. He left a permanent impression on me. He was exceptional. This brave man showed he was reliable and duty driven, the qualities needed to be a hero firefighter.

There was another fire in a private house where the occupants had made a makeshift bedroom in the attic. When the firefighters arrived, they found the house fully engulfed in flames on the first floor. The conditions on the second floor were dangerous. From the street, a bystander shouted, "There are children in the attic!" Immediately, without hesitating, the firefighter assigned to the outside vent position[1] raised a portable ladder up to the most dangerous place in the house, the attic, surrounded by smoke and flames, and carried out two children, ages three and four, unconscious. He had no choice but to act, and he did not hesitate—another act of heroism. A comparison of these two fires points to one difference: the known life hazard. If we add the two trapped children to the first fire, that fact instantly intensifies the situation, demanding we get to the children no matter what.

The first example, while just as dangerous, is less urgent because I, a trained firefighter, am the only life hazard that the probie is aware of. He can determine his pace as he looks for other victims using common sense. The second incident gives no option. The firefighter, deciding to enter that attic, knew it was a matter of life and death, and so, without hesitating and at great personal risk, he proceeded and saved two lives—that more clearly demonstrates exceptionalism by what is at stake. If he does not go, people die; if he does go, he might die. I have no doubt that the first firefighter would have done the same thing; he just didn't have to. What's most important for us is to give it our best effort.

✳ ✳ ✳

Heroes Aren't Found on Thrones

The need for models in a healthy culture is a necessary part of the education of each new generation. They should be identified in every display of human activity, ideally with the first and most important models being your own parents. Because of my background as an NYC firefighter, I have focused on heroism. However, what we call "heroism" should be expanded. Heroism is displayed when parents meet life's challenges and are models for their children. Even life itself can be viewed as heroic, whether we are talking about the disabled, handicapped, sick, or otherwise. However, the backdrop of risk that a firefighter experiences helps put it all in perspective because there are no famous firefighters, just people willing to sacrifice, risking their own life for the welfare of a stranger. That image connects American Exceptionalism, Christianity, and one of its main attributes—sacrifice.

Today, we are calling everyone a "hero" except the real ones. Heroism is being advertised as strength rather than sacrifice. The media, protected by the Constitution to inform the people, have made news a soap opera of sensationalism due to the lure of short-term profit and power, so that rather than respect, much energy is applied to the destruction of heroes without any thought as to the consequences. So often, news is the story that brings them down to earth, the story that teaches they are sinner rather than saint. The frequency and tone of reported scandals concerning soldiers in our military is one area that comes immediately to mind. Associated with disgusting stories like that of Lieutenant William Calley in Vietnam, who gave the order to kill Vietnamese villagers, or the Abu Graib prison scandal in Iraq, heroic men and women return home to resume their lives not expecting the disdain often shown and never hearing any acknowledgment for their sacrifices.

No one enjoys being humbled; however, Christian humility is actually different. Through humility comes the inspiration for us to do more, as we applaud the accomplishments of others. We need this inspiration if we're to be exceptional, and we need each other if the country is to be exceptional. It has always been the collective sacrifices of Americans that made America great. It is not necessarily unanimous input but people uniting freely around a cause, not waiting for everyone, but instead accepting the help of like-minded people to accomplish a goal. In this way, freedom of association has empowered our country.

"Every monument erected to perpetuate the memory of our heroes and statesmen ought to bear evidence of the economy and simplicity of our republican institutions in the plainness of our republican citizens, who are the sovereigns of our glorious Union, and whose virtue is to perpetuate it. True virtue cannot exist where pomp and parade are the governing passions."[2] (Andrew Jackson)

Prior to the explosion of media via Internet and cable, people freely talked about whom they considered to be their hero. For example, I always stood in awe of World War II hero Audie Murphy. The thought of him, after his best friend was killed, running up a hill with a borrowed machine gun to attack a better-positioned Nazi brigade is astonishing, but climbing into a burning German tank and using its gun on the enemy before it exploded, prevailing over 240 enemy soldiers, was all surreal to me. It is this surreal nature of heroic exploits that draws not just modern people, but people throughout human history to love heroes. It is important to recognize them because they encourage people to aim higher. Emulating the example of heroes, average individuals achieve, and some rise from their obscurity and do great things.

Since we are creatures that learn by example, we must continue to both appreciate and make use of those examples of achievement to fulfill our own vocations. As social creatures, we form associations precisely to fill those areas where we ourselves are deficient. My wife read to me a piece by author Joyce Meyer that bolsters the point:

> **"A lot of people never do anything because they cannot do everything . . . If you confidently step out and do your part, God will surround you with people who have the gifts and abilities that you don't have. However, when a person lacks confidence, quite often they cannot receive help from other people. They are too busy making comparisons to receive the help God has sent them. Insecurity and lack of confidence will steal the wonderful life that God has planned for you. It causes us to be jealous of and resent those who we should appreciate. You don't have to be prepared to do the entire job by yourself, just prepare yourself to do the best that you can do and remember that God will add what you don't have."[3]**

*   *   *

Why Is Heroism Important?

Heroism is important because it is the enemy of tyranny, suffering, and evil. Satan recognizes this power of the human spirit, namely heroism, as one of his greatest obstacles because it has the potential to spread, leading people to endure personal suffering for the common good. Having witnessed it (heroism) firsthand as an NYC firefighter, I know it does not begin with the anticipation of fanfare and glory. In fact, it is common folks who are the most dramatic heroes, people aware that despite their best efforts, things might go horribly wrong, who know there is very much to lose personally, but even more at stake if no one acts. Heroism is the "high bar" of achievement, but, unlike achievements that have accompanying reward, it also carries with it the very real prospect of tragic personal loss.

The impact of great deeds on a society comes as much from their example of sacrifice as their achieved purpose. What motivates the hero does not need to be known for their actions to inspire us. They (heroic deeds) encourage people facing daunting circumstances to persevere and prevail. The passion and death of Jesus Christ are the ultimate examples of all self-sacrifice. Christianity points us to true purpose while at the same time reminding us to fight our own evil inclinations. When Jesus becomes the principal model for us, we begin to embrace a sense of duty to our fellow man.

We are social beings. Our very purpose is to mirror the goodness of God by helping each other. Absent the purpose of helping our neighbor, we are left only with helping ourselves. If we assume that human beings are meant to live in society, then self-centered narcissistic behavior must be seen as destructive to that end. Unique talents that are hidden from others are meaningless. If Michelangelo locked every work of art he made into a vault, what purpose would they serve? Why would he have even bothered to create them in the first place?

We are the most fulfilled when we are in the service of others. In the book of Genesis, God created Adam and said it is not good for the man to be alone.[4] He created Eve as the helpmate of Adam. Part of the lesson: Life cannot be lived alone. The woman, created as helpmate to man, in the same way, needs man to be a helpmate for her. Expanding that thought, we learn about compassion and sacrifice in our relations, whether with our family or our spouse, and take what we learn as "helpmate" there to our neighbor in solidarity as fellow human beings. From this perspective, family is critical to a strong cohesive society. The exercise of compassion in the family strengthens our ability to show compassion to others and the confidence that we can make a difference. Thus, strong families, where children are naturally bound to their mother and father, and mother and father are then bound to each other, become the nuclear cells of healthy prosperous societies, infinitely stronger because what has been learned about serving others is naturally passed on to everyone.

*   *   *

Called to Duty

Whether we acknowledge it or not, there is a human calling to care, to exercise your strength where appropriate, to ease the suffering of one incapable of caring for himself. And when that opportunity arises, and it is your turn to help, it is never an adequate option to defer this responsibility to another. When we do, there is a cascade of unforeseen consequences.

They are led by a diminishing compassion, inevitable simply because we subconsciously make "caring" someone else's job. Ultimately, we must satisfy our troubled consciences, and when we hand over our power to help, we increase another's power over us. And when we concede our "calling to care" to the power of government, then we also concede to government the power to extract money from our pockets to act on our behalf. But worse, charity is a personal response to the needs of our neighbor. In deferring our charity to a central authority, we lose the power to define what charity is, and thus our unique individual sympathies become irrelevant, replaced by another's goals. This creates a great danger, in that many government objectives can be framed and funded as charity that are nothing of the sort, and thus do nothing more than funnel the citizen's personal assets into the hands of others.

Ordinary people, by helping their neighbor in small ways, are the bedrock for the American society we call "exceptional" and are the indispensable heroes who will be responsible for continued American Exceptionalism. One summer, my daughter Patrice was in the hospital in the children's ICU. She was in a panic over receiving a needle. The nurse called her by name very calmly and looked at the needle. She said, "Is this what the fuss is all about?" Then she said, "Wait here a minute, Patrice, I want to show you something." A moment later the nurse re-entered the room and showed her a huge needle, explaining, "I have a little girl your age in the other room that has cancer and has to receive this needle every day. I think you can handle this little needle, don't you?" They both began laughing, and it got done. I can't imagine what it's like to face these sick children every day. This is an example of the small daily heroism that occurs so many times every day all across the country. An honest look at these obscure heroes is both inspiration and witness, and their example is a sure way to restore America as the "city upon a hill"[5] for a world that surely needs one. Without them, or, even more important, without the compassion and charity they exemplify, the compassion and charity that accompany exceptionalism and excellence, "America the Beautiful" will no longer be recognizable. The costs attached to delegating our compassion to others (or worse to the government) are high indeed.

My wife, while a special education teacher, had a job several years back with the severely handicapped. She has remarked many times how fulfilling that job was because the people she worked with were so inspiring. They were exercising their compassion daily in the work they chose, and the residual benefit was a feeling of self-worth and accomplishment. Similarly, anyone working at Ground Zero amid the devastation could not help but notice the incredible outpouring of compassion demonstrated by New Yorkers who were inspired to help. It is human nature that when people see the disadvantaged and the afflicted, they want to help; anything else is unnatural. It is the difference between seeing things as inconvenient to you and seeing that what you can do can ease another's suffering.

In contrast, there are numerous stories around the globe where medical practitioners, on their own, have euthanized patients because they have decided there is no quality of life. These doctors and nurses decide their patients' lives no longer have value. Yet, what is our purpose for being? The poor, the lame, the elderly, etc. give us a great gift because they are the only means by which certain talents are drawn out! The less fortunate bring out the very best in people. Their needs and shortcomings bring out talents and spirit in others that would otherwise be unseen, and their witness inspires others to charity. These caregivers are some of the best examples of heroes in our midst.

⁎ ⁎ ⁎

The Cost of Heroism

Who are we calling heroes today? Anyone can come up with a list of names, but do they really measure up to true heroism? When I was a boy growing up in the Bronx, boys were encouraged to have heroes. Yet, having them serves no purpose if their example does not display true heroism. This begets the question: What is true heroism? While all heroic acts are accomplishments of a high order, not all accomplishments, great or small, are heroic.

My father knew I loved baseball and used that as a teaching opportunity. He told me about the great baseball legend Ted Williams, who learned how to be a fighter pilot in World War II, finally putting his skills to work in the Korean War, earning an Air Medal and two Gold Stars for his efforts but also missing the five best years of his renowned baseball career. He distinguished between athletic achievement and heroism, impressing upon me that the most important achievement of Williams's life was his personal sacrifice. The difference between great accomplishments and heroic acts is simple. Accomplishments are a manifestation of the gifts you have been given by God, while true heroism must involve the sacrifice. There is always a cost attached to it. Like a wild fire, heroic actions in a time of turmoil can inspire a nation, and conversely, cowardice unfortunately can lead the masses into hopelessness. After the attack on Pearl Harbor, men lined up outside recruiting stations all across the country. They

107

collectively interpreted the attack not simply as an attack on our government, but as an attack on their way of life. This is because American patriotism has never been perceived as loyalty toward a leader or to a government, but as loyalty to our Constitution, which defines our God-given rights and provides a framework to ensure them, to protect them from their perpetual foe—Satan. Attacks on America are more than an attack on our home; they are attacks on the most valuable possession—freedom.

On September 11, 2001, the New York City Fire Department responded to the World Trade Center attacks and firefighters continued without rest in the days and months following, tirelessly engaging in the rescue and recovery operation, endangering their own health in the daunting task to find survivors. Simultaneously, a multitude of our fellow New Yorkers converged on the devastation, providing all forms of support from firefighting to debris removal, even to the point of simply being there to feed us, clothe us, and cheer us on. Somehow, that spirit has been replaced by uncertainty and a contagious uneasiness about what America is really about. More upsetting, I have heard some in academic circles show disdain toward our Constitution. If the people's allegiance to our founding documents is lost, so too will America's sense of mission.

Prudence, justice, fortitude, and temperance—the cardinal virtues of the Christian tradition—also energize, encourage, and promote acts of heroism. Can the American heroism we have come to expect thrive without America retaining her Christian identity? These virtues are demonstrated in charity and are more effective than personal motivations to inspire a climate of national heroism.

The hard work of survival is a daily struggle that calls for small acts of heroism, which, when encouraged, can lead to a return of American greatness. This is not a prideful greatness but a greatness that benefits humanity because it provides a model for all nations to follow, and they follow it directly to Almighty God. It is, rather, a humble greatness that recognizes the interdependence of all Americans, and, even better, all citizens of the earth.

"If any man will come after me, let him deny himself, and take up his cross, and follow me."

Life is work, pain, trial, error, and disappointment, and we do not retreat from it but instead persevere through it. We gain in strength knowing as the motto goes, "No pain, no gain." My high school science teacher used to say, "The human body is the only machine that gets better the more you use it." The premise also applies to us collectively. Let's endure America's trials together.

Jesus said to his disciples: "If any man will come after me, let him deny himself, and take up his cross, and follow me." (Matthew 16:24). We are not taking up the incredible burden of his Cross but instead our cross, unique and personal, like no other. It is the cross that is carried every day of our lives. It is the work of living. Every chore and effort required to live, performed in consideration of our neighbor to the best of our ability, can become a small heroic undertaking if we give it in charity. The cumulative effect is to grow in virtue and extend the influence of one's efforts. The goal is not to create a utopia but to apply your talents to those less fortunate. Jesus said:

"For the poor you have always with you: and whensoever you will, you may do them good: but me you have not always." (Mark 14:7)

109

8

OUR MOST VALUABLE ASSET

THE MOST VALUABLE ASSET OF ANY NATION IS ITS PEOPLE, but for that asset to contribute the most, people must be free and secure in their property. In America, exceptionalism is about the people and it comes from their guaranteed liberty and not from any inherited excellence. Once that guarantee disappears, the 'pursuit of happiness' that is the source of exceptionalism quickly erodes as freedom erodes, so that the gifted in the population find it harder and harder to distinguish themselves.

We are a melting pot because many different people all share in the same set of beliefs outlined in the Declaration of Independence. But you can't be a melting pot if you don't melt! Think of a fruit salad; the orange is not an apple, the apple is not a peach, the peach is not a banana. They are recognized, not as a salad, but remain what they are. Put them in a blender though, and they become one, even though all the ingredients are still the same. The mix of many different societies is only a strength if they unite around a common overarching goal. It is not about identifying all the different parts, but instead identifying what is the same, the common goal. One step America must take to recover exceptionalism is to stop labeling ourselves as anything other than 'American.'

Our history is characterized by oppressed people who have been coming to these shores because their worth in the eyes of God is identified in our Declaration and protected by the Constitution. My paternal grandparents came from Ireland, and my maternal grandfather and great grandmother came from Ukraine and Poland, respectively, in the early 1900s. They never became wealthy, but they felt like they hit the jackpot when they made it here. I can remember my relatives trying to name the counties of Ireland during a family party. My grandmother came in. Obviously annoyed, she said, "This country fed and found us. We're American now; why don't you try to name the fifty states?!"

Yet, today, fewer and fewer people see their country as a blessing; meanwhile, the Constitution, which was intended to safeguard us from future tyranny, is being challenged by varied segments of society. Whether it be left-wing media, educational institutions, or those intoxicated by power in our government, the Constitution is under fire, and it must be defended by "we the people" whom it serves and protects. It specifically defines and limits authority but more importantly makes them accountable for their actions. In tyrannical regimes, dictators refuse to be accountable to anyone. But here, our liberty is the prime focus of our founding documents because the authors believed it came from the one true God.

The United States of America has been blessed with unprecedented progress, not because of some genetic superiority but rather because we exclude no one. Our founding documents harness the power of the human spirit because they protect everyone. This notion that no one person has more value than another is indicative of the Christian flavor of America. Jesus Christ died for all and faith in him was deeply held by a predominance of the founders. The good shepherd leaves the ninety-nine to find the one who has gone astray because that lost one is just as important as the rest. If a nation enslaves or exploits its people, how can the people prosper? Western Europe has embraced Socialist goals. Its fatal error is in reducing human flourishing to material equality, thus reducing unique people into biological units. The dignity of each human being is assaulted because the autonomy of the individual is lost as he is forced to comply with a standard set by another. Having grown up in and worked in poor neighborhoods, I know it is not true that the poor are simply lacking the ability to acquire things. Many of my friends' families were content with what they had, did not aspire for fame or wealth, and wanted nothing from anyone. We shouldn't underestimate the power of propaganda to alter perceptions—it can turn the satisfied into the disgruntled. Attitude is everything. Something can be looked at as either an obstacle that stops them or a challenge that emboldens them. Many times, friends would joke about firefighters, saying they're running in while everybody else is running out, but that is the difference—firefighters see the fire as a conquest, a test of their mettle.

I have had a couple of friends point to Scandinavian countries as an example of flourishing Socialism. I am not going to cover the myriad reasons why this is false. Suffice it to say that having physical possessions is not the same as having freedom. The spiritual assault in the following current example will say enough. In Sweden, homeschooling is illegal. Christer and Annie Johansson considered this an assault on their parental rights and chose to homeschool their son Domenic. In

June 2009, after harassment, fines, and court battles, the parents decided to relocate to Annie's home country of India with Domenic, then seven years old. They were on the plane waiting to take off when Swedish police boarded, seized the seven-year-old, and put him into foster care where he has been since. A Swedish appeals court permanently transferred custody of Domenic to foster care and terminated Christer and Annie's parental rights in December 2012.[1] For the Johanssons, no amount of economic security will give them peace.

The narrative has been set by the modern progressive movement to reduce Christianity to a philosophy. This makes the Christian faith one of many competing philosophies rather than what it is, namely, faith in Jesus, the Son of God. He models for humanity perfect heroism, sacrificial love and mercy. He alone has the ability to do this because he is God. The founders believed this, and they left our country a formula for excellence. The underlying Christian tradition at the heart of American history is that formula. When the people come first, heroes and leaders emerge from every walk of life, including elected government because it is of, by, and for the people. As Andrew Jackson eloquently stated, our Republican citizens are "the sovereigns of our glorious union."[2] If America focuses her energy on preserving the God-given liberty of her people, then it will rediscover the real source of her wealth, the unlocked talent of her people. But this will only happen as long as America continues to cherish her founding. Any disregard of our founding can only stem from a real contempt for what someone stands for, which is essentially the rights of the common man. The inspiration of the Founding Fathers was a morality drawn from their prevailing Christian faith, as contrasted with the present American pursuit of secularism that denies the real and ancient American mind that made possible exceptionalism and our heroes. That faith and our heroes are gifts from a generous God who approved of our cause.

*   *   *

The Father of Our Country and American Exceptionalism

Republican governments are overthrown in one of two ways: 1) gradually by slow encroachment and dissolution of designed protections, or 2) immediately by invasion and war. We maintain a powerful military, prepared to deal with the latter, but have become vulnerable to the former because we are not holding politicians accountable to the law. In fact, today it is blatantly circumvented, as with the Clinton email scandal or the overreach of the Department of Justice in its political investigations. Not holding politicians accountable to the law quickly erodes legal protections—it confers power on those who already hold office that the rest of us do not share. Politicians are stretching the meaning of the Constitution to serve personal ends and as the trend continues unchecked, it leaves citizens with less and less ability to stop it, until finally the system serves the powerful rather than the citizens. This trend also becomes a tool for our external enemies, whoever they may be, to exploit and coerce our government. Religion defines morality and virtue, giving America natural boundaries for behavior that were intended to be part of our system of law and are indispensable if America's Constitution is to succeed in protecting liberty.

George Washington, the first U.S. president, has always been called the father of our country and rightly so, yet this is an understatement. Our first president was the personification of America, the true son of the republic. History proves that no one more dramatically placed duty before self than he did. Aware of the human flaws that challenge liberty, in his farewell address, George Washington spoke to us about the dangers that threaten our Constitutional government.

> "But the Constitution . . . is sacredly obligatory upon all
> . . . All obstructions to the execution of the laws . . . , with
> the real design to direct, control, counteract, or awe the
> regular deliberation and action of the constituted
> authorities . . . are destructive of this fundamental princi
> ple, and of fatal tendency.

> "They serve to organize faction, to give it an artificial and
> extraordinary force; to put, in the place of the delegated
> will of the nation the will of a party. . . associations of the
> above description may now and then answer popular ends,
> they are likely, in the course of time and things, to become
> potent engines, by which cunning, ambitious, and unprin
> cipled men will be enabled to subvert the power of the
> people and to usurp for themselves the reins of govern
> ment, destroying afterwards the very engines which have
> lifted them to unjust dominion."[3]

Washington illustrates the inevitable scheming for power that will undermine the individual liberty originally intended. Prophetically, this is precisely what is playing out today. Minority factions, including the established parties, are successfully pitting Americans against each other and separating the people from the government. The Affordable Care Act dictated what an insurance company must pay for. Even the Little Sisters of the Poor found themselves on the wrong side of this law. Similarly, the Supreme Court's decision on marriage in June 2015 (*Obergefell v. Hodges*) puts traditional marriage adherents on the wrong side of the law as seen in the bakery case in Oregon.

Hard-working Americans are losing pieces of their liberty every day, a liberty won by heroic blood during the revolution. The same degree of heroism demonstrated in 1776 is necessary today and will be tomorrow if America is to preserve her liberty. It will take that kind of unwavering heroism to restore what is lost. Fortunately, the courage necessary is nurtured and made firm by our Christian roots. Unfortunately, America is dismissing those roots, but the cure is simple: Turn back and acknowledge God.

When we realize our own faults, we take the difficult first step toward exceptionalism. Completely relevant today, Washington, our first president, wary of human nature, prophetically described how tyranny masquerades itself as security. He is a mentor, not just of politics, but also threats to liberty, describing just how our naiveté and fears will be exploited.

Today's faction is Socialism covertly planted in our government institutions but more importantly in the fourth estate, the press that must sell it to us, the electorate. Essential information is either excluded, tainted, and/or altered to distract the citizenry and move public opinion in one direction just as a herdsman moves cattle.

Take an honest look at the effect of polling data prior to an election. The press eagerly publicizes this data even though it provides no useful information. Polls neither inform the voter of a candidate's platform nor establish his competency. However, they are very effective at making qualified candidates look hopeless, so that campaigns can be made to appear hopeless. It takes enormous courage to defend truth when the power of the news media is your foe. In the same way, modern authors are busy diluting our heroes, past and present. Their heroism is deliberately overshadowed by dramas created by digging up with great fervor their personal sins.

People need heroes but are fascinated by villains. Socialists sell the political concept of equality of outcomes that naturally denies exceptionalism by denying gifted people the fruits of their labor. The media assist by demonizing the founders, happy to take them down from their pedestals and become their equal. Americans, like no other people, must remember where they came from. Our Christian heritage is infused in our government, and it gives us an eternal perspective on our liberty and its adversaries, both physical and spiritual. America hasn't changed; it is being changed by a force that is both internal and external, physical and spiritual.

* * *

What Is Freedom?

"If we were carelessly to identify freedom with power, we obviously would nurse tyranny, exactly as we land into anarchy when we equate liberty with lack of any restraint."[4]
— **F. A. Hayek**

I have polled many West Point cadets on the meaning of the word *freedom*. Their answers are typically variations of the same theme: "the ability to choose for yourself what you want to do." Sometimes they add the idea of "respect for others" or "within the bounds of law." But these descriptions are lacking. Who decides the bounds of law? They do not give clear guidelines for when one person's freedom infringes on another's.

Let's look at freedom from two extremes. One extreme would be the complete absence of freedom—tyranny and slavery. The other extreme is completely unbridled freedom where everyone is in a state of chaos. This is anarchy. Neither of these two polar opposites is acceptable but does that mean we find real freedom somewhere in the middle? Is that all it takes? If that is the case, where is the 'middle' ground? Every one of us, even with the best of intentions, is going to draw the line somewhere else. For you it will be in one place, for me in another, for your neighbor yet another. And by allowing the 'line' to be drawn by men, we necessarily become vulnerable to every evil that men are capable of. To avoid this, the 'line' that establishes the boundaries of human freedom must come from outside of Man. This is what makes America unique. The Declaration of Independence affirms that God draws the line which leaves us free of Man.

While mankind is inclined to abuse power, often powerful people can be defenders of liberty. When those with power acknowledge a duty to their fellow man, that power is instantly converted from a threat to an asset. In fact, freedom depends on powerful people to oppose evil. Christianity, by encouraging the strong to help those less fortunate, gives America the formula for exceptional government by teaching the appropriate use of strength.

I remember listening to a speech given by former Arkansas governor and presidential candidate Mike Huckabee while campaigning in 2008 to an unusually hostile group of students at a college in upstate New York. He said, " . . . government is only necessary to the extent that you are unable to govern yourself." Huckabee had not even finished the sentence before he was met with boos from throughout the audience. I, on the other hand, loved the succinct association between self-control and government. His comment suggests three ingredients to good government: first, the need for self-discipline; second, government that goes no further than necessary; and third, a standard by which a culture governs itself. Without a standard of right and wrong, of good and evil, it is impossible to teach self-discipline because we have no way of knowing what that discipline should look like. Presidents have often commented on the revelation of the Gospel as the standard of life as shown in the following quotes:

> "The general principles on which the fathers achieved independence were . . . the general principles of Christianity." (John Adams)

> "No nation has ever yet existed or been governed without religion. Nor can be. The Christian religion is the best religion that has been given to man, and I as chief magistrate of this nation am bound to give it the sanction of my example." (Thomas Jefferson)

> "The teachings of the Bible are so interwoven and entwined with our whole civic and social life that it would be literally impossible for us to figure to ourselves what that life would be if these teaching were removed." (Teddy Roosevelt)

> "America was born a Christian nation—America was born to exemplify that devotion to the elements of righteousness which are derived from the revelations of Holy Scripture."(Woodrow Wilson)

> "American life is built, and can alone survive, upon . . . [the] fundamental philosophy announced by the Savior nineteen centuries ago." (Herbert Hoover)

> "This is a Christian nation." (Harry Truman)[5]

> "It cannot be emphasized too clearly and too often that this nation was founded, not by religionists, but by Christians; not on religion, but on the gospel of Jesus Christ. For this very reason, peoples of other faiths have been afforded asylum, prosperity, and freedom of worship here." (Patrick Henry)[6]

Being a Christian nation, however, does not mean that America is immune to evil. The lust for power transcends particular religions and cultures. To support fairness and justice, laws must flow out of truth and apply to everybody equally. Dr. Martin Luther King, Jr. quotes Saint Augustine in his famous "Letter from Birmingham Jail":

"One has not only a legal but moral responsibility to obey just laws. Conversely, one has a moral responsibility to disobey unjust laws. I would agree with Saint Augustine that 'An unjust law is no law at all.' "[7]

How do we know any law is unjust except because it contradicts God's law? Unjust laws abuse power and freedom. That is why enemies of America, in fact enemies of freedom, attack Christianity, because they simultaneously attack both God and America. In the 1980s, Pope John Paul II saw public displays of Christianity banned because they challenged state authority.

Unbridled, Americans benefited from growth and prosperity never before seen in the world. How stupid can we be to abandon a formula proven to work for a formula (Socialism) proven to fail. Nonetheless, since the mid-1800s when the evils of Socialism were formally introduced, our love for our founding principles has gradually waned.

"Let us, my friends and fellow-citizens, unite all our endeavors this day to remember with reverential gratitude to our Supreme Benefactor all the wonderful things he has done for us, in a miraculous deliverance from a second Egypt—another house of bondage."[8]

— Elias Boudinot,
signer of the Declaration of Independence

PART III
THE
CHRISTIAN
NATION

9

JUDEO-CHRISTIAN HEROISM

WHY WOULD A SOLDIER IN A FOXHOLE WILLINGLY DIVE ON AN INCOMING GRENADE? Does he win or lose? What inspires him to sacrifice himself? His heroic action is best understood in light of the sacrifice of Jesus Christ who died for us on the Cross. That's what gives it meaning. Through faith, he knows that this is not the end for him . . . it's only the beginning. That is why feats of bravery fill our history from the *Mayflower* to today. Consequently, how would that history be different if we were not a Christian nation?

"No man taketh it away from me: but I lay it down of myself, and I have the power to lay it down; and I have power to take it up again." (John 10:18)

This brand of heroism distinguishes itself from the heroism of the ancient pagans. Their concept of heroism was identified with exceptional strength and tied to victory. They prided themselves in their conquests and were lauded for those conquests by their people. Their reward was immediate, but there was nothing to be gained in losing. You do not normally hear stories of ancient pagan heroes choosing a losing cause. This is not to say that there weren't incredible personalities willing to take incredible risks for fame and fortune. However, the spread of Christianity has added a new dimension to courage so that every single living person is a potential hero.

The prideful strength of the past doesn't equal the inner strength that comes from knowing the truth about our eternal future. Judeo-Christian heroism involves more than just war. Before, there was no value placed in losing, the victorious were remembered, and the defeated were forgotten. But for the Christian, evil is to be opposed at all times. The glory of the victory was replaced by the glory of God.

There is no more dramatic demonstration of the difference between the two than the epic battle between David and Goliath. The heroes of the pagan world were always men with exceptional strength. Goliath was a giant warrior and with every "heroic" victory, he glorified himself. David, on the other hand, believed that more important than winning or losing was to fight for the one true God. The slightly built David, just a boy, slew Goliath, not with the sword but with the sling. The complete heroism of David is affirmed when he accepts this insurmountable battle, not when he wins it. Christians naturally see the 'Davids' of the world as heroes regardless of whether they win or lose.

"Thou comest to me with a sword, and with a spear, and with a shield: but I come to thee in the name of the Lord of hosts, the God of the armies of Israel, which thou hast defied. This day, and the Lord will deliver thee into my hand, and I will slay thee, and take away thy head from thee: and I will give the carcasses of the army of the Philistines this day to the birds of the air, and to the beasts of the earth: that all the earth may know that there is a God in Israel. And all this assembly shall know, that the Lord saveth not with sword and spear:

for it is his battle, and he will deliver you into our hands." (1 Samuel 17:45–47)

David is unconcerned with his odds, only that he puts God before himself. He is willing to be a martyr should it come to that because there is no other choice that is acceptable. Physically winning a fight has less to do with courage than it does with ability. The cause behind the fight, and the defense of the weak and innocent adds a new dimension that inspires courage. How much of the fortitude necessary to finish the fight comes from knowing what you are doing is right? My father always believed that if you are in the right, let nothing stop you. And that is the gist of it. Do you really lose, even in defeat, when you are defending a just cause? Or do you lose, in reality, when you knowingly do nothing?

Despite the propaganda today, this is the reality of America's rise on the world stage. Our most decorated soldier on the battlefield, Audie Murphy, resembles more of a David than a Goliath, and so do his achievements on the battlefield. And he's just one of many American heroes in a trail of American heroes dating back to our Revolutionary War. They were inspired by the cause of American liberty because of their Christian upbringing. And every time since, when freedom was threatened, whether by slavery, Communism, or genocide, our people understood the founding documents, identified the threat, and fought. The country was willing to stand up to any nation to defend her liberty. But what happens when the challenge to our freedom is not obvious? What if it comes from amongst us here at home?

Today, we are rapidly deserting our Christian founding in favor of secularism and, at the same time, America is experiencing stagnation. The first half of American history is just the opposite. As I indicate throughout the book, the miraculous explosion of America on the world was accomplished by a nation that identified itself as Christian. Just like King David, they were confident in the battle against their Goliath, Great Britain, and that their efforts would produce future blessings for America. John Witherspoon, signer of the Declaration of Independence, said:

"... It would be a criminal inattention not to observe the singular interposition of Providence thereto in behalf of the American colonies . . . Has not the boasted discipline of regular and veteran soldiers been turned into confusion and dismay before the new and maiden courage of freemen in defense of their property and rights? In what great mercy has blood been spared on the side of this injured country! . . . While we give praise to God, the supreme disposer of all events, for his interposition in our behalf, let us guard against the dangerous error of trusting in or boasting of an arm of flesh. The Holy Scriptures in general and the truths of the glorious gospel in particular, in the whole course of Providence, seem intended to abase the pride of man and lay the vainglorious in the dust."[1]

"While we give praise to God, the supreme disposer of all events, for his interposition in our behalf, let us guard against the dangerous error of trusting in or boasting of an arm of flesh."
-John Witherspoon

✳   ✳   ✳

A Wimpy Religion?

I was driving a guest of the United States Military Academy at West Point, a retired veteran of thirty years, and we began to talk about current events. The two of us hit it off well and we agreed that many of our political woes were due to a collapse of our national morality. We talked about the economy, about foreign policy, and about our government.

At some point during the conversation, I connected our national woes to the abandoning of our Christian principles. I was a little surprised by his response. He said, "I agree with you, I'm Christian, too, but I don't think Christianity is coming back because it is kind of perceived as a wimpy religion." I said, "How so?"

He answered, "Because it talks about turning the other cheek and forgiveness, I think it's looked at around the world as being weak."

My answer was Christianity is more than two thousand years old. If Christians were not bold and strong, Christianity would have been exterminated in its infancy by the Roman persecution. Secondly, the witness of Christian martyrs is not one of weakness. The sacrifice of their lives for the faith is a testimony of courage that is extraordinary and awe inspiring. It conjures up for me the image of a church that is both indestructible and heroic. One idea is not supported—namely, that these martyrs are cowards or that their faith was weak. While he agreed with me in the end, his comment stuck with me. Christ's very genuine courage was displayed when he sacrificed His own life. The idea that death is not the end but the beginning makes the sacrifice of Christian martyrs understandable and clarifies life and the value of sacrifice. America, the nation, fought not simply to be liberated from England, but to liberate every individual. We are not a Christian nation because Christians live here; instead, our nation's Christianity is seen in our method of self-government that is an exercise of your individual liberty. The American Revolution is a revelation on liberty which has successfully inspired many parts of the world to adopt representative government. And, consequently, the world is a much freer place than it was two and a half centuries ago.

Separation of Church and State?

America's modest beginning depended on industrious people whose self-sacrifice quickly built a world power. In contrast, today's consumerism stifles those qualities by focusing on what we do not have. Its use of ads and media does not consider doing without and is naturally self-centered. This is a distinct contrast from the Christian culture that places value in the virtue of temperance and self-control because, for profit's sake, it encourages excess and waste. Unfortunately, it is Christians who embraced this modern consumerism that is in conflict with Christian values.

Our founders were not only devoted Christians, they were people who acknowledged divine intervention. They used the broad term *Creator* and thus were able to unite the many Christians sects to form a nation of God-given freedom.

Numerous court cases throughout the course of two centuries remind us that Americans have always considered this to be a Christian nation. In 1861, Justice Allen of the Supreme Court of the State of New York made the following statement:

"Christianity is part of the common law of this state, in the qualified sense that it is entitled to respect and protection as the acknowledged religion of the people . . . The claim that the constitutional guarantees of religious liberty are inconsistent with the recognition of Christianity as the religion of the people, is repelled by the known character and history of the framers of the Constitution. They would not sacrifice their freedom or their religion. They and their forefathers were the champions of both."[2]

Religion in America is not simply anyone's concept of reality. Its definition is narrowed by the Declaration of Independence to be about the Creator who endowed all of us with unquestionable rights without prejudice. No definition of God, where He withholds his gifts from some, is compatible with America. Religion and the Creator are inseparable, and freedom of religion cannot be confused with freedom of merely a belief system. Much of the controversy today comes from this misuse of the First Amendment that the founders meant for the God who carved out the Ten Commandments.

"The Bill of Rights contains no grant of privilege for a group of people to destroy the Bill of Rights. A group—like the Communist conspiracy—dedicated to the ultimate destruction of all civil liberties, cannot be allowed to claim civil liberties as its privileged sanctuary from which to carry on subversion of the Government."[3]
— **Dwight Eisenhower**

The founders, as well as the majority of early Americans, believed in Jesus Christ. The challenge was to find a way to unite the various Christians who had formally been divided and were actively antagonizing each other. Today's secular progressives advance a false picture, portraying the founders as deists rather than Christians, the goal being to remove the opposing influence of Christian culture from their secular agenda, yet the opposite is true. William Federer, renowned American historian, in a lecture about Jefferson, Franklin, and Deism,[4] pointed out that Deism had a different meaning than how we understand it today. The Encarta North American English Dictionary's definition of *Deism* is:

"A belief in God based on reason rather than revelation and involving the view that God has set the universe in motion but does not interfere with how it runs."[5]

Dr. Federer states that the concept of deism then was different. It essentially affirmed the belief in Jesus Christ but not the need for a formal church. He pointed to the founders' call to prayer and fasting, along with their belief that lives should be modeled after Jesus. He noted that in the modern definition, prayer would have no purpose if God wouldn't interfere in their affairs.

There is a more important point. When you research the histories of these men, you find that their families had strong affiliations with various Christian congregations. For instance, George Washington's great-great-grandfather, Reverend Lawrence Washington, was an Anglican minister in Essex, England. It's hard to imagine that they would wholeheartedly abandon the faith of their childhoods. However, since the various Christian sects were hostile to each other, it would be difficult to gain the trust of the people if they were connected with any particular religious sect. Thus, it was expedient for them as representatives of the new government to be deists and thus not affiliated with any particular church.

Further, the Founding Fathers, to whom we owe this freedom, did not just privately believe in God. They felt Him act on their behalf. George Washington, in fact, believed it was incumbent upon him to show public gratitude which he did in this address to the nation.

" . . . it would be peculiarly improper to omit in this first official Act, my fervent supplications to that Almighty Being who rules over the Universe, who presides in the Councils of Nations, and whose providential aids can supply every human defect, that His benediction may consecrate to the liberties and happiness of the People of the United States, a Government instituted by themselves for these essential purposes: and may enable every instrument employed in its administration to execute with success, the functions allotted to his charge. In tendering this homage to the Great Author of every public and private good, I assure myself that it expresses your sentiments not less than my own; nor those of my fellow citizens at large, less than either. No People can be bound to acknowledge and adore the invisible hand, which conducts the Affairs of men more than the People of the United States. Every step, by which they have advanced to the character of an independent nation, seems to have been distinguished by some token of providential agency. And in the important revolution just accomplished in the system of their United Government, the tranquil deliberations and voluntary consent of so many distinct communities, from which the event has resulted, cannot be compared with the means by which most Governments have been established, without some return of pious gratitude along with an humble anticipation of the future blessings which the past seem to presage."[6] (from George Washington's First Inaugural address)

Consider whether President Washington could say these words and, at the same time, advocate a separation of Church and State. It is obvious today that some parties, in an anti-Christian spirit of anarchy, have deliberately misconstrued what separation of church and state means for the purpose of undermining the influence of Christianity on our modern culture. There is no way that our original patriots, so vocal about their faith, intended to "tie their tongues" concerning the one reason they believed made their cause true. The Christian faith of the founders was not just demonstrated, it was announced repeatedly. Thus, common sense dictates they would not hamper but rather encourage continued public pronouncement of what they considered to be the one true faith.

Historian William Federer also discussed the origins of the term "separation of Church and State."[7] Misrepresented, it means the opposite of what we hear today. To answer the concerns of the Baptist churches in Danbury, Connecticut, Thomas Jefferson ties the position of the new government to the position of the Baptist church by quoting renowned Baptist minister and founder of Rhode Island, Roger Williams.

Roger Williams experienced the power of government over the church when, after he had been chosen as a pastor in Massachusetts, he was expelled in 1636 by Puritan leader John Cotton for his religious views. He fled to and founded the Rhode Island colony and then, in 1639, the Baptist church in America. He and Cotton debated each other in a series of published letters including "Mr. Cotton's Letter Lately Printed, Examined and Answered" in 1644 where he addressed the censoring of religious speech using the term, "Wall of Separation." Williams explains that the labors of the Church of the Jews of the Old Testament and the Christians of the New Testament were separated from the "wilderness of the world" by God and that when they "opened a gap" in the "wall of separation" between the Church and the world, God destroyed the wall turning His Church into a wilderness, an allusion to the many instances in the Bible where God's people were persecuted because of their sin.

To be restored it must "of necessity be walled in from the world . . . a separation of Holy from unholy, penitent from impenitent, Godly from unGodly." Jefferson's use of Williams's phrase makes clear that restraints are intended for government, but today it is used to silence Christians. Is this an accidental mistake? Silencing established moral authority (the church) is and was the goal which shaped the new modern use of the term. Jefferson is not changing the meaning of Roger Williams's analogy. If he were, there would be no reason to quote him in the first place. The quote affirms the purpose of the First Amendment to restrict government in order to protect the moral voice of the church.

* * *

The Experiment

Consider for a moment that, on December 22, 1620, the Puritans came here to escape persecution. And when they arrived, they stepped ashore and consecrated the new land to Christ and the Christian religion. Unlike the economic goals of Jamestown in the South a few years earlier, their goal centered around the Creator. The difference between these goals is critical as we take a deeper look at the progress of America, North and South, 'slave' and 'free,' and realize the battle for the soul of America that culminated in the Civil War existed in the very beginning with Christianity at the center of it. And, as we examine exceptionalism, the North, which fought against the evils of slavery, was also the wealthier and more prosperous of the two.

"The first act of the Puritans, after landing, was to kneel down and offer their thanksgiving to God, and by a solemn act of prayer, and in the name and for the sake of Christ, to take possession of the continent. They thus repeated the Christian consecration which Columbus, more than a century before, had given to the New World, and so twice in the most formal and solemn manner was it devoted to Christ and Christian civilization."[8]

Their determination throughout unimaginable hardship was born out of a personal desire to follow Jesus Christ. We owe our privileged life to the suffering they were willing to endure as a result of their faith.

"The *Mayflower* sought our shores under no high-wrought spirit of commercial adventure, no love of gold, no mixture of purpose warlike or hostile to any human being. Like the dove from the ark, she had put forth only to find rest... Every prosperous breeze, which, gently filling his sails, helped the Pilgrims onward in their course, awoke new anthems of praise; and when the elements were wrought to fury, neither the tempest, tossing their fragile bark like a feather, nor the darkness and howling of the midnight storm, ever disturbed, in man or woman, the firm and settled purpose of their souls to undergo all and to do all that the meekest patience, the boldest resolution, and the highest trust in God could enable human beings to endure or to perform."[9] (Daniel Webster)

Are American Exceptionalism and Christianity connected? My American 'experiment' is to compare, as in a petri dish, the flourishing of early America to the confusion of today's America to prove God and man collaborate to make an exceptional society.

The character of the Founding Fathers was formed by that pilgrim generation. Americans have publicly acknowledged year after year with pomp and parade what was won by the sacrifice of the previous generations. President Kennedy also remembered our roots in his aforementioned inaugural address:

> "The torch has been passed to a new generation of Americans—born in this century, tempered by war, disciplined by a hard and bitter peace, proud of our ancient heritage—and unwilling to witness or permit the slow undoing of those human rights to which this nation has always been committed, and to which we are committed today at home and around the world."[10]

He was both calling attention to the great feats of our American ancestors and reminding the nation that the battle for our freedom is a perpetual one. Critical to the success of that battle is the eternal example of heroism, Christ. Jesus on His Cross has inspired so much heroism throughout the centuries, but, most importantly, here in America, an entire nation declared, "In God We Trust!" for the first time. When we aspire to something, we model our actions after someone who has achieved it. For every Christian, that model is supposed to be Jesus who teaches:

"Greater love has no man than this, that a man lay down his life for his friends." (John 15:13)

" . . . I lay down my life, that I may take it again. No one takes it from me, but I lay it down of my own accord; I have power to lay it down, and I have power to take it again." (John 10:17–18)

10

TRUE LAW IS ABSOLUTE

AS SEEN IN THE GREAT SEAL OF THE UNITED STATES, the Founding Fathers believed God is both necessary for and desires freedom and heroism. Since 'good' coexists with evil, freedom is, for its protection, limited by law. The question is: "Whose law do we allow to limit freedom, God's or Man's?"

As far back as Cicero, the common-sense concept of eternal Truth and true law is reasonable. He connects it to its one source—the Creator and ultimate judge of all.

"True law is right reason, consonant with nature . . . It is constant and eternal; it summons to duty by its orders, it deters from crime by its prohibitions . . . We cannot be released from this law by the Senate or the people, and it needs no exegete or interpreter . . . There will not be one law at Rome and another at Athens, one now and another later; but all nations at all times will be bound by this one internal and unchangeable law, and the God will be the one common master and general of all people. He is the author, expounder, and mover of this law; and the person who does not obey it will be in exile from himself in so far as he scorns his nature as a human being; by this very fact, he will pay the greatest penalty, even if he escapes all the other things that are generally recognized as punishments . . . "[1] (Cicero)

This seems to me to be the result of real enlightenment. If people decide how to restrict people, you invite tyranny. Yet, we have traveled full circle from relative truth to eternal Truth and now back to relative truth again. The world understood enough to dismiss the thoughts of Pontius Pilate who asked, "What is truth?" for the teachings of Christ who said, "I am the Truth," only to return by way of secularism to a relative truth. Cicero knew that true law must be "consonant with nature," but when this reality opposes secular objectives, truth becomes the enemy. Modern man fights nature itself for two reasons: first, because nature judges his acts; and second, because of his own innate pride and selfishness.

"In *Lord Jim*, Joseph Conrad wrote: ' . . . no man ever understands quite his own artful dodges to escape from the grim shadow of self-knowledge.' Artful denial is a common disposition of those who will not compromise their ideology with reality, lest they be discomfited by the fact of evil."[2] (Fr. George Rutler)

In theory, justice is blind, disregarding any distinction between individuals, defined by laws designed to protect the rights of all. Our liberty is safeguarded by laws enforced by a government that is, at the same time, subject to them. They are supposed to be generated by, as Cicero states, "the one common master and general of all people." That is the purpose of the Constitution of the United States and why it should be treasured. The constant threat to free countries is in becoming vulnerable to power through the arbitrary use of laws and regulations. If it is left up to man, laws can easily become weapons. This is why their purpose should conform to eternal truths. America's laws are based on Biblical principles, and America should guard and apply her laws to check power with the same zeal she does in defending rights and freedom because unchecked power is perhaps the greatest threat to those rights and freedom. As Lord Acton famously said:

"Power tends to corrupt, and absolute power corrupts absolutely."[3]

Judeo-Christian tradition, however, provided the wisdom underlying the American experiment because it exposes not just that we are flawed beings, but that we are inclined to evil. By constantly reminding us of the existence of evil, Christianity evokes a sort of vigilance so that the enemies of our American way of life are recognized and stopped. In contrast, without the lens of Christian tradition, how do we recognize what threatens us? The Founding Fathers clearly identified the enemies to liberty, internal and external, physical and spiritual, and crafted a constitution to defend against them. They were cognizant of the evil motives of people that continually threaten the liberties of everyone.

The easiest way to evaluate our laws is by a common standard. In America, that standard is simply defined in the Declaration of Independence. The objective of the Constitution, the framework of our government, is to defend the philosophy and morality found in the Declaration of Independence that connected divine law to the rights of man. Alexander Hamilton said:

"The Supreme Intelligence who rules the world has constituted an eternal law, which is obligatory upon all mankind, prior to any human institution whatever. He gave existence to man, together with the means of preserving and beautifying that existence, and invested him with an inviolable right to pursue liberty and personal safety. Natural liberty is the gift of the Creator to the whole human race. Civil liberty is only natural liberty modified and secured by the sanctions of civil society. It is not dependent on human caprice, but it is conformable to the Constitution of man, as well as necessary to the well-being of society. The sacred rights of mankind . . . are written . . . by the hand of Divinity . . . and can never be erased or obscured by human power. This is what is called the law of nature, which, . . .being coeval with mankind and dictated by God himself, is, of course, superior in obligation to any other. No human laws are of any validity if contrary to this. It is binding over all the globe, in all countries, and at all times."[4]

It's clear from the words of Hamilton that the laws of nature referred to in the Declaration of Independence are eternal laws from God that we are not only obliged to obey, but cannot contradict. It is important to recognize that these eternal laws are not merely a matter of opinion but instead the entire premise on which this country is built. The Constitution is designed to protect the truths in the Declaration of Independence. Its moral force was demonstrated "Four score and seven years"[5] later when the words "All men are created equal and endowed by their Creator . . . " could no longer be ignored and the hypocrisy of slavery was abolished. The Constitution relies on the Declaration of Independence to give it purpose and authority. It is its moral compass. By recognizing God as master, Americanism assumes we are free from men and thus protects the individual from the powerful so they may follow God's commands. This is the recipe for an exceptional people. Is a locomotive a slave to its tracks because it cannot choose its direction? Or is the train only free if you remove the tracks? Nonsense! The train either goes nowhere or crashes without the tracks . . . and so does a human being.

As our nation moves to secularism, it must also move away from God as lawmaker replacing him with man. Government without God as its head quickly degenerates because the attraction of power that comes with government is an unavoidable temptation.

"There is no safety for honest men except by believing all possible evil of evil men. Those who have been once intoxicated with power and have derived any kind of emolument from it can never willingly abandon it."[6] (Edmund Burke)

The founders soberly considered man's inclination to evil when they deliberated on the constructs of this unique government because of their knowledge of history and what is taught in Christianity about our corrupt nature. They were well aware of the temptations instrumental in the destruction of past republics because they were raised in a tradition that taught them of the common weakness in every man. By identifying the seven deadly sins of pride, envy, wrath, sloth, greed, gluttony, and lust, Judeo-Christian tradition shows the Constitution what it guards against.

"Without morals, a republic cannot subsist any length of time; they therefore who are decrying the Christian religion, whose morality is so sublime and pure . . . are undermining the solid foundation of morals, the best security for the duration of free governments."[7] (Charles Carroll, signer of the Declaration of Independence)

Jesus was asked, "Which commandment is the first of all?"

" . . . Jesus answered, 'The first is . . . the Lord our God, the Lord is one; and you shall love the Lord your God with all your heart, and with all your soul, and with all your mind, and with all your strength. The second is this, 'You shall love your neighbor as yourself.' There is no other commandment greater than these." (Mark 12:29–31)

This call to love is nonnegotiable; it is a commandment! Jesus Christ calls everyone into service, both to God and to man; thus, for Christians, the service of God doesn't include the harming of man. That service often requires courageous effort and is rooted in charitable love. America's roots in Christianity are demonstrated from the very first moments of our existence as a distinct people. Our earliest American ancestors, the Pilgrims, were so driven to create a community that abided by this commandment that they were willing to leave everything they knew to make it happen. The roots of exceptionalism are rightly traced back to the inspirations of the pilgrims to build a Christian society.

Why did these people permanently leave the comfort of home for the unknown? They traded everything they knew for the dream of freely worshiping God. Courage marks the beginning of America and her rise among nations, but there was another, more important supernatural component. The settling of the colonies is a statement about the human spirit . . . and the human soul. As Jesus said, "The spirit is willing, but the flesh is weak." The great football coach Vince Lombardi once said, "Fatigue makes cowards of us all." But when the disciples asked, "Who then can be saved?" Jesus answered, "With men this is impossible, but with God all things are possible." (Matthew 19:26)

If we are looking for freedom from men, we must be a slave to God. But if we seek freedom from God, we will be a slave to Man. The laws of nature referred to in the opening paragraph of the Declaration of Independence identify a plan God has for his creation that we cannot reject without consequences because people are a part of that plan, but this is not slavery as we understand it. Life has a universal purpose as depicted in my analogy a few pages ago. The locomotive is a great invention that includes tracks, but it crashes if I choose to remove the tracks. Mankind is like the locomotive. The Creator our founders acknowledged puts mankind on 'tracks' for our own good so that we can reach our destination—Him. If we refuse to use them, we inevitably crash.

The Christian heroes in each generation focus on the lives and freedom of others. Their work in turn inspires others to likewise sacrifice and to do more than they wanted to or ever thought they could. The collective efforts of the American colonies demonstrate better than any what can be achieved this way. So many writings from the Founding Fathers and the patriots of the revolution are proof of what encouraged them.

". . . That God who presides over the destinies of nations will raise up friends for us."[8]
— **Patrick Henry**

"The world is very different now. For man holds in his mortal hands the power to abolish all forms of human poverty and all forms of human life. And yet the same revolutionary beliefs for which our forebears fought are still at issue around the globe— the belief that the rights of man come not from the generosity of the state but from the hand of God."[9]
— **President John F. Kennedy**

* * *

Freedom from Ourselves
Perfect freedom doesn't exist unless we are free from ourselves. One of the gifts of the Spirit is called the gift of temperance. It means to practice moderation in all things and to

resist indulging appetites and passions. As in the extreme of addiction, anything that you cannot say 'no' to enslaves you. "Truly, truly, I say to you, everyone who commits sin is a slave to sin." (John 8:34)

When the founders identified our God-given right to the "pursuit of happiness," they too were alluding to the value of temperance. The enlightenment philosopher, John Locke, so influential in our founding, defined the "pursuit of happiness." He said:

" . . . we are, by the necessity of preferring and pursuing true happiness as our greatest good, obliged to suspend the satisfaction of our desires in particular cases."[10]

Overindulgence of anything is not just potentially harmful but it also distracts and even prevents you from achieving your goals and as such is an impediment to exceptionalism. Your desires replace God as the priority of your life. Saint Paul warns:

"For many . . . conduct themselves as enemies of the cross of Christ . . . Their God is their stomach; their glory is in their shame." (Philippians 3:18–19)

Christians serve God by using their unique gifts to serve others. As Jesus said, "Amen I say to you, as long as you did it to one of these my least brethren, you did it to me." (Matthew 25:40) The work of denying ourselves is the hardest work of all. Its pursuit, in and of itself, is a heroic endeavor because we are inclined to take the easiest path. And, personally, once I saw the gratitude of the people I helped as a firefighter, I became addicted to service. That feeling of good is never known in a life of self-gratification.

"I am the way, and the truth, and the life. No one cometh to the Father, but by me." (John 14:6)

The patriotism of Joseph Warren, who died at Bunker Hill on June 17, 1775, was a result of his faith.

"If you perform your part, you must have the strongest confidence that the same almighty being who protected your venerable and pious forefathers, who enabled them to turn a barren wilderness into a fruitful field, who so often made bare his arm for their salvation, will be still mindful of you, their offspring."[11]

Heroism and temperance are spiritual, born out of love of neighbor. Love of neighbor is more than merely good citizenship, it inspires the sacrifice seen when we fulfill our roles in society as father or mother, firefighter, or teacher, etc. This ingredient of true love makes people care. And this caring is then reflected in our work ethic and our compassion. It makes us become part of one another's lives, fulfilling the deep social characteristic in us. Real love is required for real heroic action. A true hero truly cares about his neighbor.

For a long time after 9/11, we went to funeral after funeral on our off days. I remember how hard that was on me; 343 firefighters had died, and as their remains were discovered, funerals were arranged. But I remember one day in particular. I had been to two funerals that morning and I looked at the department orders and saw there was another that afternoon in Staten Island. I was considering whether to go home or go to another funeral and I finally said, "You have to go." When I got there, I saw only the family and about twenty-five firefighters along with one bagpiper from the FDNY bagpipe band. I began to remember the funerals I had gone to prior to 9/11 with thousands of firefighters lined up to pay their respects and a procession of fire apparatus, bagpipers, and dignitaries. A sad feeling came over me and I felt very guilty that

I had debated whether to go or not. It didn't seem fair that he couldn't have the same honors as so many had before him . . . but I was so glad that I went for the family's sake. They were very pleased to see those of us who were able to make it. It made me realize how important it is to go the extra mile, to extend yourself a little more than you want. You just don't know what that means to someone until you do it.

11

SLAVE TO GOD, FREE FROM MAN . . . FREE FROM GOD, SLAVE TO MAN

"For so is the will of God, that by doing well you may put to silence the ignorance of foolish men: As free, and not as making liberty a cloak for malice, but as the servants of God."
— 1 Peter 2:16

I F ASKED, MOST OF US WOULD SAY WE STAND FOR FREEDOM; I'm sure of it. We would also probably say that we believe in the rule of law. Yet, since laws are prohibitive, and since they are written and enforced by human beings, to protect freedom rather than threaten it, they must be based on universal principles.

Have you ever pulled out a board game that you hadn't played in a while, remembering the fun and great times you had while playing it, only to find that the directions were missing? Was everybody overjoyed at the newfound freedom of not being constrained by rules? Of course not. Depending on the game, the missing rules can make playing chaotic or impossible. Trying to make up your own rules denies you the same enjoyment you remembered. Life is the same way. Life's rules have been put in place before we came to "play." They come from the Creator and not from humanity.

Civilized society becomes confident in a system of law only when it knows that the law is not arbitrarily applied. America begins defining the rule of law right in the Declaration of Independence when it acknowledges the "Laws of Nature and of Nature's God" as the basis for all law. Saint John says, "All things were made by Him: and without Him was made nothing that was made." (John 1:3)

Jesus, the Son of God, said, "You call me Teacher and Lord; and you are right, for so I am . . . " (John 13:13). He continues, "No longer do I call you slaves, for the slave does not know what his master is doing; but I have called you friends, for all that I have heard from my Father I have made known to you."(John 15:15). Jesus, describing Himself as 'master,' implies that we are slaves, but what God does here is flip the whole meaning of the word *slave* on its head. We are not being told to obey His command to avoid punishment but instead to obey to be called His friend. "This is my commandment, that you love one another as I have loved you . . . You are my friends if you do what I command you." (John 15:12-14)

In human slavery, the master's commands benefit the master, but Jesus is teaching us that God's commands *benefit us*. But it is even more intimate than that. Jesus connects the role of master to that of teacher by showing us what to do by way of example: "If I then, your Lord and Teacher, have washed your feet, you also ought to wash one another's feet. For I have given you an example, that you also should do as I have done to you." (John 13: 14-15). He led by example from the washing of the Apostles' feet to His laying down of His life for His friends.

The truth is we are either slaves to God or slaves to man—there is no in-between! The one master loves while the other hates. When we submit to the commands of God, we discover a master who designed us and cares for us. By rejecting God, we are opposing our very nature and begin to give in to and embrace all the temptations that come with freedom from God, eventually heading out of control. Then we truly become a slave to man. That is obvious every time we see anyone who overdoes any pleasurable thing, and more dramatically (and tragically) in addictions.

That is why Jesus says, "My yoke is sweet," (Matthew 11:30) because His commands are what we are meant for—they are natural. The enslaving yoke of man, the gift of the devil, makes us see our neighbor as an obstacle because we put our own selfish needs first. That yoke is hard because it is contrary to our nature as social beings. The true Master loves the heroes he has created; the false one hates them. The honest search for and embrace of God's purpose is "freeing" because we discover what really satisfies us.

At about five o'clock in the morning, on September 13, 2001, after about twenty hours at Ground Zero, I completed what amounted to a futile search for victims of the 9/11 attack on the World Trade Center. I was walking down West Street, completely numb, when people on the sidewalk began clapping. Deli owners were giving out sandwiches. A chiropractor even had her table in the street to give adjustments to rescue workers (I remember some long lines for her).

While I was stunned by the devastation all around me, I was also moved by the heartwarming solidarity shown by so many people there. I guess everybody felt attacked and everybody needed to be involved, just like when a family member is attacked and the rest of the family comes to their aid. They forget about the quarrels they might have had and unite. On September 13, 2001, I had family all around me. My fellow Americans from all fifty states became my fellow New Yorkers!

Firefighters predominantly are responding to a call to help their neighbor, but on this day, it was obvious that the country, too, felt that call and responded with small acts of heroism in the form of charity. Yet, instead of this sense of unity growing (after all, we know the threat of terrorism still exists), it has been eviscerated. We have illogically embarked on a course of division that unwittingly contributes to the goals of the original 9/11 assassins. America is at war with itself, dividing itself into small factions. What was formerly the proud melting pot has been converted into the home of the hyphenated American. Our neighbor has become offensive and tolerance has virtually disappeared. How do we unite if we can't look to God for answers?

* * *

Our Strongest Ally

I am very concerned with the growing division in America. We were never united by a shared ancestry or genetics, but rather by a shared Creator. The spirit of America, the zeal for liberty, was confidence in God. This relationship was clear from the outset. In the debate over the feasibility of war with England, Patrick Henry reminded his fellow patriots of their strongest ally.

"We must fight. I repeat it, sir, we must fight. An appeal to arms and the God of hosts is all that is left us . . . "[1]

His passion doesn't just reveal *his* faith. He was able to appeal to his counterparts because they shared a common faith. In the pragmatic debate over war, Patrick Henry would not have considered his personal faith to be a compelling reason for fighting the Revolutionary War. It had to be shared by all of the Virginia delegates to whom he was speaking. How could they in turn expect to inspire the people unless they, too, were people of faith? This spiritual relationship is witnessed over and over. George Washington remarked:

"History can hardly produce such a series of events as has taken place in favor of American opposition. The hand of Heaven seems to have directed every occurrence."
- **Elbridge Gerry**

"I am sure that there never was a people who had more reason to acknowledge a divine interposition in their affairs than those of the United States . . ."[2]

Benjamin Morris remembers John Adams:

" 'I always consider,' said he, 'the settlement of America with reverence and wonder, as the opening of a grand scheme and design of Providence . . .' "[3]

Dramatically, Elbridge Gerry, signer of the Declaration of Independence, in a letter to Samuel Adams on December 13, 1775, expresses similar sentiments:

"History can hardly produce such a series of events as has taken place in favor of American opposition. The hand of heaven seems to have directed every occurrence."[4]

In times of battle, people must be unified. In unity there is strength. Division causes disintegration, and when things disintegrate, they disappear. And, as history has proved, if America cannot reunite, she too, will disappear. Moreover, this country wasn't founded simply to make the colonies independent of England. The previous quotes point to an American spirit that united around God. The colonies didn't just combine forces, they united under a banner of freedom, willing to sacrifice, firmly believing they were aided by God.

Honoring God gives twofold grace; first, in the form of wisdom and, second, in the form of his miraculous aid. America has been blessed and the question is: "What are the consequences for disregarding the source of those blessings?" The Old Testament tells of the prophet Jonah warning Nineveh to repent or be destroyed. Fortunately for them, the king led the people in repentance, putting on "sackcloth and ashes" and they avoided that destruction.[5] Can we avoid such an end absent the very same commitment?

We need a similar recognition of our errors and, just as the Ninevites, humbly acknowledge the authority of the Creator just as we see throughout the Declaration of Independence. That is the only change of course that qualifies us to lead again. Modern America has not just ceased to publicly acknowledge God, she has shown a disdain for Him altogether, dismantling the institutions like marriage that have always been respected by the Church and removing references to His authority. Marriage has been changed, and statements like 'In God we trust' are being challenged, all to appease small segments of the population. Without making the connection between our prosperity and 'Providence,' humility disappears, and the power that should be ceded to the Divine is ceded instead to authority. Is that what America is? Are we defined by radical freedom or as protector of rights given by the supreme authority of God Himself? President John F. Kennedy said:

" . . . there is little value in insuring the survival of our nation if our traditions do not survive with it."[6]

To preserve the liberty for which our ancestors fought, we must preserve the Judeo-Christian origin of our law. What is in a name? A country can call itself "America," but if it does not protect individual liberty, it is not America. In our march toward secularism, we are losing God, and in so doing we are also leaving behind absolute truth, defined morality, and the divine law, all of which bred a national confidence because it clearly marked our path, one we could return to any time we (America) are faced with hardship. Civil law built on God's Law is sound law. Our nation must put on sackcloth and ashes and humbly acknowledge our weakness without God in order to return to glory.

Rejecting our founding is regressive. If how we treat our neighbor is the hallmark of Christian civilization, then, the less concern we have for our neighbor, the less civilized we are. *Progressive*, the popular catchphrase in the academic and political arena, is identified with open-mindedness and tantamount to reform. Progressives attach themselves to many causes with the message, 'raise the standard of living of the forgotten poor.' But while the poverty line is rather subjective, slavery is not. A subtle truth is that while many classified as living in poverty are happy, no one who is enslaved is happy! Free choice must always be part of 'progress.' Therefore, measures aimed at the good goal to raise the standard of living must never trump individual liberty. The success of the Judeo-Christian conception of liberty can be seen by examining the growth, until recent years, of the United States. The only way we can be truly progressive is to return to policies that both demonstrate growth and are good—that put the happiness of our neighbor first. C. S. Lewis, in a profoundly simple way, identified the trap of progressivism.

> "We all want progress. But progress means getting nearer to the place where you want to be. And if you have taken a wrong turning, then to go forward does not get you any nearer. If you are on the wrong road, progress means doing an about-turn and walking back to the right road; and in that case the man who turns back soonest is the most progressive man."[7]

Heroic men and women are born in every generation. However, to see them, we need the humility to distinguish between the truth that "all men are created equal" and the other truth about ourselves that "created equal" does not imply that we are equally gifted. Thus, the key to identifying Americans as equals in the Declaration of Independence is that we are, in fact, created first and that the one doing the creating is also the one giving the gifts.

The solely American statement that all men "are endowed by their Creator"[8] distinguishes America from other nations and is the one truth that our country must always affirm to be consistent with our founding. The honest search for and subsequent submission to truth is being laughed at by modern man. Today truth is relative, a kind of antique that society thinks, once discarded, will free him from unnecessary constraints to his wishes.

"There must be religion . . . Vicious rulers, chosen by a vicious people, turn back the current of corruption to its source. Placed in a situation where they can exercise authority for their own emolument, they betray their trust. They take bribes. They sell statutes and decrees. They sell honor and office. They sell conscience. They sell their country. By this vile practice they become odious and contemptible."[9] (Gouverneur Morris of New York)

History testifies to the powerful exploiting the weak. From Caesar to Attila, unchecked evil will forever use the strong to tyrannize the weak. It must be vigilantly checked by good people. Hard times invite tyranny when a society lacks the strength to persevere through those times. The Great Depression closely following World War I caused such despair that the Germans were willing to follow a strong figure to avoid further hardship, thus inviting the evil of the

Nazis. It has been the same throughout time. The only protection is to know what is good and beware the corrupting nature of power. The Israelites of the Old Testament told the prophet Samuel:

"Give us a king to judge us." Samuel was told by the Lord to "hearken to the voice of the people . . . For they have not rejected thee, but me, that I should not reign over them."

Samuel warned them that a king will take your sons, your daughters, your fields, etc. and,

"You shall cry out . . . and the Lord will not hear you in that day." (1 Kings 8:4-19)

We must make sure that we never ask for a king—it was hard enough to get rid of him the first time.

* * *

Why Does It Matter?

Why should we be free? When are we free? The athlete says, "No pain, no gain" because fruitful choices are rarely easy choices. They involve virtue and integrity, fortitude, and perseverance. People choose to be free, not because it is easy or because it is safe. On the contrary, it always requires work, suffering, and sacrifice. We must fight to be free because, as creatures made in the image of God, we must be free as He is free. This is why it is a heinous crime to enslave a man or for a man not to cherish and defend his freedom. Freedom, heroism, and Judeo-Christian tradition thus become linked to each other in the American Experiment because freedom must always be guided by what is good and right. As George Washington stressed in his farewell address:

" . . . Give to mankind the magnanimous and too novel example of a people always guided by an exalted justice and benevolence. Who can doubt that, in the course of time and things, the fruits of such a plan would richly repay any temporary advantages, which might be lost by a steady adherence to it? Can it be that Providence has not connected the permanent felicity of a nation with its virtue? The experiment, at least, is recommended by every sentiment, which ennobles human nature. Alas! Is it rendered impossible by its vices?"[10]

Doing what is right often means forgoing some immediate reward for the sake of another. There is an inner strength that must be used to successfully resist short-term gain, and a degree of wisdom is required to see the greater reward. Everybody's work is magnified when it is done for God because the purpose of the work is greater and also because God Himself has been involved. This explains the rapid progress of the United States; nothing else, genetic or otherwise, is particularly unique. The difference is not that America was saintly, devoid of dubious characters, but in the national "atmosphere" produced by our protection of freedom. There is a link between freedom and initiative; more of the former produces more of the latter.

Because of the numerous examples of Christian government in Western Europe over the centuries, people argue that America is not unique in its Christian values. The one glaring difference: Europe depended on a good Christian monarch. Thus, Europeans were only guaranteed to last for a generation. There was no assurance that the future would produce similar benevolence. The American founding is just the opposite. The Constitution was guaranteed for the future, while the elected leadership was made replaceable. If the Constitution is followed, the system will continue to protect liberty regardless of the morality of any particular individual.

In my years as a firefighter, the most common attribute that I saw in the people I worked with was the satisfaction they derived from touching lives in the community in a positive way. It is a mistake to focus only on how a free society enables the wicked because it just as successfully enables the givers in humanity.

A fruitful life means sacrifice and perseverance. Six-time undefeated world karate champion Chuck Norris said:

"I get the thrill of victory. But, I never got the agony of defeat . . . Although I did lose several times in my climb up the competitive ladder, let me share with you my philosophy on winning and losing along the way. Through years of competition, I found that the only time I ever really lost was when I did not learn from that experience. I would say to myself that I may have lost this time, but I will never lose the same way twice. It helped me not to get discouraged or upset. Or as the great Vince Lombardi explained, 'It's not whether you get knocked down; it's whether you get up.'"[11]

This is about getting up, not being helped up. We are meant to learn from and get strengthened by every trial. The fledgling United States learned from human history and grew strong as a people through the trials of colonial subjugation and subsequent war, vowing not to live that way again. They codified a government designed to repel those past abuses with defenses such as a free press to hold the government accountable.

159

PART IV

FREEDOM AND AMERICAN EXCEPTIONALISM

12

REAL FREEDOM

"Finally, true freedom is not advanced in the permissive society, which confuses freedom with licence to do anything whatever and which in the name of freedom proclaims a kind of general amorality." [1]

— **Pope John Paul II**

S O THEN, HOW DO WE USE OUR FREEDOM? What we do with freedom determines whether our communities prosper or disintegrate. Let's contrast two small towns. The first is filled with people who work feverishly to be prepared for any possible need so as not to have to rely on their neighbors for help. The second community is filled with people who work feverishly to build cooperative spirit and unity in their neighborhood. Which one of these two communities will fare better in the aftermath of a devastating tornado?

The first one has varied results depending on how competently each household prepared. Some families might well end up completely destitute with nowhere to turn. The second one, on the other hand, is characterized by families that immediately look outward to join their efforts at restoring their entire neighborhood. Together, no one is left behind.

The outward-looking individual is not self-absorbed, collapsing in on himself, judging everything he does by his own needs. Instead, he or she is moved by the needs of the people around him. These outward-looking people are the everyday heroes in our midst. Christ himself commanded his disciples to sacrifice for each other, as He himself sacrificed his own life for them.

Alexis De Tocqueville had the unique opportunity to contrast two different violent revolutions that spawned two different outcomes. He says:

"Every revolution has more or less the effect of releasing men to their own conduct ... When equality of conditions succeeds a protracted conflict between the different classes ... , envy, hatred, and uncharitableness, pride, and exaggerated self-confidence seize upon the human heart, and plant their sway in it for a time. This, independently of equality itself, tends powerfully to divide men, to lead them to mistrust the judgment of one another, and to seek the light of truth nowhere but in themselves. Everyone then attempts to be his own guide and makes it his boast to form his own opinions on all subjects."[2]

A struggle with a vision of freedom defined by Christianity, which is shared by a predominance of the people, is unifying. De Tocqueville here alludes to the French Revolution: "Equality of conditions arising out of envy produce disunity, very much like today." Equality of conditions is at the heart of Socialism and must therefore be repelled if we are to remain a United States.

A wise man once said no one chooses to remain ignorant when he can know the truth. If so, then what could lead a man to accept a lie? The second threat to real liberty is personal weakness. If a man is led by his passions, if he is not inspired to control them, then he will listen to voices that justify his illicit action and dismiss those that condemn them. True freedom is not a license to do anything you want; that is simply a lack of restraint, a lawlessness, and immodesty toward your fellow man. George Weigel, following the thought of Saint Thomas Aquinas, describes freedom:

> "Freedom is the capacity to choose wisely and to act well as a matter of habit or, to use the old-fashioned term, as an outgrowth of virtue. Freedom is the means by which, exercising both our reason and our will, we act on the natural longing for truth, for goodness, and for happiness that is built into us as human beings. Freedom is something that grows in us, and the habit of living freedom wisely must be developed through education, which among many other things involves the experience of emulating others who live wisely and well."[3]

Many years ago, I worked a night tour in Ladder 28 in Harlem, working for someone who needed off. I introduced myself and did a roll call. That's when a senior chauffeur told me we had an inexperienced crew, two from the engine and a probationary firefighter. He suggested calling the battalion to swap for a more experienced firefighter but I told him, "We'll be fine." No sooner had the words left my lips than an alarm came in for a fire in a multiple dwelling. Immediately, the dispatcher cut in on the voice alarm, saying, "We are receiving numerous calls on this . . . you are probably going to a working fire." Rarely does the dispatcher speak directly over the voice alarm, so we knew we had something.

The dispatch ticket showed us as second-due to arrive while my friend E. J., the lieutenant in Ladder 30, was first-due. While en route several blocks away, a firefighter banged on the window and pointed to his right. Over the roof of the building across the street, I saw flames engulfing every window on the top floor of the five-story occupied multiple dwelling. As we began to anticipate attacking heavy fire conditions and the possible life hazard for a top-floor fire, I heard E. J. give the signal 10-84 (arrived on scene) followed by 10-75 (working fire) and asked for a second alarm because he was being met by fire at the front door. I thought he must be at a different fire since I was looking at a top-floor fire.

When I arrived a minute later, I saw the fire had completely engulfed all five floors of the building and began to anticipate removing numerous victims. My position as 'second-due' was to search the floors above the fire, but heavy fire conditions were beyond the apartments, in the stairwell, public hallway, and each landing. With the wood stairs on fire themselves and E. J. and his companies, Engine 59 and Ladder 30, in an apartment on the first floor, I waited while second-due Engine 68 stretched their hoseline and then had them extinguish the stairs to the second floor. Because of the extensive damage, I called for a portable ladder to be put on the stairs. I proceeded to climb to the second floor when I felt the stair landing drop an inch or two. I was worried about the stairs collapsing into the fire behind them and motioned to the other firefighters who had also started up the ladder. They could not understand me because our face masks muffled our voices, so I turned and hustled up the remaining rungs of the ladder as quickly as possible. Thankfully, we all made it upstairs. Conditions upstairs were even worse with fire everywhere and the walls crumbling, but 68 and 59 extinguished enough of the hall to move in to quickly knock down fire in the second-floor apartment as other companies began to arrive on the scene. So much debris had fallen on the next staircase that, as the water hit it, the stairs became like a mudslide. The extreme pressure of the hoseline had them sliding down the stairs, and the engine company was making no progress. Conditions began to deteriorate and the second floor began to reignite. It was an anxious moment . . . there just seemed to be more fire than we could handle. That's when I received a pat on the shoulder. The battalion chief, a salty Vietnam veteran about sixty years old, responsible for the whole operation, was no longer in the street. He was now standing next to me with dense black smoke all around us, making him nearly invisible. Through the blackness you could see the dark red flames rolling along the ceiling and lapping up the staircase. He said, "You better get them to make a push or we're going to lose the building." Trying to look as relaxed as he, I said, "How'd you get up here?" The chief was not supposed to be in that spot with the downstairs apartments still not under control, but he was compelled to come up because of the dangerous conditions.

Calmly, he said, "The fire escape." We were in a very dangerous spot, and I dodged a lot of ceiling plaster falling and was worried about the whole ceiling collapsing. The chief quickly assessed the situation, knew how little time we had, and left his command post to see what we were up against. He fought his way up with us as we went one floor at a time until the fire throughout the building was completely extinguished.

He did not have to be there—but he was. The more serious the fire, the more this man felt he needed to be right there in it to make sure he could share his experience and expertise. The chief was a model for giving your best effort. When we seek human excellence, we naturally want to emulate those who are examples of that excellence, and he will be for me one of those examples.

*　　*　　*

Courage and Freedom

It takes courage to face the unknown and possible failure; so, there's a heroic nature in the embrace of freedom. Yes, it actually takes courage to prefer freedom. Timid souls are afraid of their own choices and afraid to make commitments because of what might go wrong. It becomes easier to allow others to make those choices for you. If this sounds familiar, it is probably because it is all around you. Security is being sold as protection from hardship, and its value has been exaggerated.

"There is a certain enthusiasm in liberty that makes human nature rise above itself, in acts of bravery and heroism."

-Alexander Hamilton

It is a fact that a free society is by nature unsafe. Ben Franklin's comment bears repeating:

"They who can give up essential liberty to obtain a little temporary safety deserve neither liberty nor safety."[4]

In man's pursuit of the unknown, or the untried, he expresses both courage and freedom in exploring new paths. And when despotism prohibits man from living according to his own choices, it takes collective courage to free him. Freedom feeds courage, and then courage defends freedom.

The difference between a political climate that is conducive to individual freedom and one that consolidates authority is that freedom may produce as many solutions to problems as there are people, while a centralized power does not encourage solutions that do not come from it because it can never share power. When a brilliant person's ideas are used, that person had the 'power' to change his environment. The free society quickly becomes exceptional because of the explosion of ideas; the Totalitarian, Communist, or Socialist society stagnates because of the suppressing of ideas. People need to be encouraged to take risks and that happens when a society eagerly looks forward to and is ready to reward personal success. The Alexander Graham Bells and the Thomas Edisons are not encouraged in Totalitarian, Communist, or Socialist society. They are coerced, and their enthusiasm is lost.

For example, it is often proposed that government programs be adopted to connect people to jobs via planned job training. This path takes the focus away from each person's uniqueness and puts it on agendas set by the government and the vision of the powerful. What if the government had the authority to tell Albert Einstein to become a farmer or William Shakespeare to become a sailor? The free choice of individuals to direct their efforts to jobs they really want provides the motivation for colleges to provide that training, thus creating a healthy competition between colleges and universities.

The community that is free is filled with confident men and women. That confidence becomes contagious, spilling over into the rest of society. Each achievement then gives motivation to greater things because they are personal. That doesn't happen in Socialism, Communism, or Totalitarianism because the achievement belongs to the state.

"There is a certain enthusiasm in liberty that makes human nature rise above itself, in acts of bravery and heroism." (Alexander Hamilton, *The Farmer Refuted*, February 23, 1775)

* * *

What Are We Responsible For?

President John F. Kennedy had one common theme to his presidency, namely, the responsibilities of the American citizen. His inaugural address became famous for the challenge:

"Ask not what your country can do for you, ask what you can do for your country."

This is the mature look at the world that the citizen should take, and it calls for the courage not to shirk one's duty. It is a heroic call, not just to a few but to all! Kennedy, in 1963, gave a warning about the responsibility we have to vigilantly protect our rights:

"But this Nation was not founded solely on the principle of citizens' rights. Equally important, though too often not discussed, is the citizen's responsibility. For our privileges can be no greater than our obligations. The protection of our rights can endure no longer than the performance of our responsibilities. Each can be neglected only at the peril of the other."[5]

This is the power of unity. He meant to inspire individuals to freely be part of the whole, to make a nation, and it reminds us that citizenry is a responsibility. Now, let's contrast that philosophy to America today by looking at one of President Obama's executive orders capping annual student loan payments. He then used it as a moment to accuse Republicans of preferring to help big oil rather than helping students embroiled in debt, telling them, "Good luck."[6] The order and the statement, while being political gamesmanship, are also harmful to American strength for two reasons. First, it is vitriolic toward fellow Americans (Republicans), dividing our government and forgetting who it serves. Secondly, it is purposely deceitful, ignoring the real issue: our responsibility as citizens. This is not a question of telling students, "You're on your own." But it is about ignoring the fact that we all should be accountable for our actions. Justice in society depends on accountability and the honest student will acknowledge not only that his debt was his choice, but also that it is no one else's responsibility. Loans, while needing regulation to protect us from the unscrupulous lender, are contracts between free people that must be protected. We must demand responsibility from ourselves, because our privileges can't be greater than our obligations. There are two sides to every agreement and we can be on either side, borrower or lender, at different times in our life. We will pay a greater price with our liberty if we condone public interference with private agreements!

* * *

Is It Liberty or Leisure?

America today is preoccupied with pleasures. The amount of screen time people spend on their devices, TVs, and computers has reached epidemic proportions, and the abuse has become a topic of debate. The salaries of entertainers and athletes have skyrocketed, reflecting the willingness of fans to pay whatever it takes to see their favorite stars. The amount of time Americans spend at work has decreased with shorter work days and work weeks. And might it all be at the expense of duty?

This country was created, grew, and expanded through blood, sweat, and tears on an untamed continent. Before the invention of television and radio, a person had to intentionally and actively look for vices. With a little bit of willpower, I might resist the temptation. But the more you are exposed to your weaknesses, the more inner fortitude it takes to resist them. This is the biggest downfall of technological progress. Whenever someone is preoccupied, he is going to miss the things happening around him . . . or worse. If any particular pleasure becomes an addiction, everything else becomes secondary. And today, technology has made it possible for perversions, like child pornography, that wouldn't have made the light of day in the past, to permeate our modern society.

America is rapidly relinquishing her leadership status, choosing instead to follow the world. And she is no longer distinguishing herself by virtue of her sublime national creed. Instead, she is plunging into new depths of narcissism. The ramifications are being seen in how we express our freedom. Human lives are being destroyed through abortion and euthanasia, many times as a matter of convenience, and the biological human family is being made irrelevant. To lead a world gone astray—in essence, to lead them to respect true freedom—we must rediscover our founders' reliance on God because reliance on God delivers a certain confidence that underlies sound choices.

As indicated by our absurd national debt, America's maxim has been changed from "earn what you have" to "buy now and pay later" or, even better, "buy now and let somebody else pay." The "talking heads" and politicians manufacture issues facing a stumbling America, in the process never acknowledging the real core problems. Politicians are focused on looking forward to the next election; they are not seeking to do their job, just to keep their jobs. They create the problem and then offer the solution, yet the problems never go away. But those small lies simply cover up the big lie: The nation does not need God. Regardless how impressive technology is, it cannot deliver us from our human weaknesses. We need to be diligent in recognizing our enemies, beginning with the prince of lies who infiltrates our lives through many venues.

"He was a murderer from the beginning, and he stood not in the truth; because truth is not in him. When he speaketh a lie, he speaketh of his own: for he is a liar, and the father thereof." (John 8:44)

Real Freedom

"Liberty means responsibility. That is why most men dread it."
— **George Bernard Shaw**

As a New York City firefighter, it was obvious to me that there was a model of courage built into the occupation. Unlike most dangerous professions, as you advance through the ranks in the Fire Department of New York, you're still a firefighter, entering the fire or emergency first. Thus, comfort and safety are not a motivation for seeking promotion. No honor is received that removes firefighters from the perils of the job. But, if you think about it, this is really the only way it should be. There is nothing exceptional about that—the promotion was the honor. The fire still needs to get put out, and everybody there should contribute regardless of rank. This applies to a community as well. The more people who feel an obligation to help their neighbor, the better off the community is, and, for the Christian, it is understood that all people are obligated to help their neighbor.

Today, the false heroes we prop up do not just confuse what is truly heroism but popularize role models that are inherently damaging to society. So, we have to be very honest about what we want our country to look like, not in appearance, but in action and in purpose. Then the role that our Christian roots and our Declaration of Independence play in our success will become clear, as will our responsibilities to our country and our neighbor.

In the Gospel, Jesus is very clear that we will be judged, not only on how we offended our neighbor, but on how we helped our neighbor.

"Then the King will say to those at his right hand, 'Come ... inherit the kingdom prepared for you from the foundation of the world; for I was hungry, and you gave me food, I was thirsty and you gave me drink, I was a stranger and you welcomed me, I was naked and you clothed me, sick and you visited me, I was in prison and you came to me.' Then the righteous will answer him, 'Lord, when did we see you hungry and feed you or thirsty and gave you drink?'... And the King will answer them, 'Truly, I say to you, as you did it to one of the least of these my brethren, you did it to me.'"

But Jesus continues:

"Then he will say to those at his left hand, 'Depart from me, you cursed, into the eternal fire prepared for the devil and his angels; for I was hungry and you gave me no food, I was thirsty and you gave me no drink, I was a stranger and you did not welcome me, naked and you did not clothe me, sick and in prison and you did not visit me.' Then they also will answer, saying, 'Lord, when did we see you hungry or thirsty or a stranger or naked or sick or in prison, and did not minister to you?' Then He will answer them, 'Truly, I say to you, as you did it not to one of the least of these, you did it not to me...'" (Matthew 25:34)

America today is marked by uncertainty and a contagious uneasiness fueled by distrust of leadership. We see this uncertainty in the vehement opposition between Democrats and Republicans and in polls indicating Americans are extremely dissatisfied with the direction of government. We are losing our sense of mission because the mission, to protect our God-given rights, is meaningless without God. America is right to be uneasy; we have been disconnected from our roots so that our current path does not reflect our founding principles.

13

IS SUCCESS OUR GUIDE?

S OME ATTRIBUTE THE FOLLOWING QUOTE TO ALBERT EINSTEIN: "The definition of insanity is when someone does the same thing over and over again seeking different results." Regardless of whether he said it, there is some truth to it. Aren't the results the barometer of success or failure? From this perspective, the American Revolution must be deemed a complete success, not just because the war was won, but more importantly because the colonies succeeded in forming a new government that protected individual liberty for its posterity and because that new-found liberty reaped rewards they could never have imagined.

Now contrast present-day America. Our nation is no longer considered the freest country on the earth (which I will discuss more in depth in the last chapter). The nation is essentially bankrupt. Laurence Kotlikoff, writing for *The Economist*, in his article, "America is Bankrupt," said:

"The US has a fiscal gap, the present value of all its future spending (including servicing its official debt) less all its future taxes, of $202 trillion—almost 14 times GDP . . . To close the US fiscal gap would require raising all federal taxes, immediately and permanently by almost two-thirds!

. . . Focusing on the debt . . . is straight out of 'The Emperor's New Clothes' . . . if enough people start looking at . . . the infinite horizon fiscal gap, they will realize that the US is bankrupt—not in 30 years, not in 10 years, not in 5 years, but today . . . when that happens the crisis will follow immediately."[1]

Americans themselves are heavily in debt, with the old topic of concern, credit card debt, being eclipsed by student loan debt. Division amongst our citizens is obvious. Americans no longer identify themselves as Americans, but rather some kind of subset.

Finally, religious liberty, the prime motivation for our first settlers at Plymouth Rock, placed first in the Bill of Rights by our founders, is disappearing. The public square, where a civilized society should demonstrate its civility by welcoming debate, and where people show respect for each other, has replaced religion with irreligion, and put religious expression in a sort of 'solitary confinement' wherever it clashes with politically correct revision of timeless truths. In the process, civility has been replaced by hostility.

Amidst this decline, we have advanced Socialist policies, proven to fail, that serve to create envy between the rich and the poor in order to cash in politically. Why are we entertaining ideologies that have proven dangerous and fail to deliver what they promise? Socialism is always accompanied by Totalitarianism because someone has to have the power to take wealth in order to redistribute it. From the Soviet Union to Venezuela today, people are hurt by Socialism. The Founding Fathers were specifically fighting Totalitarianism, so to embrace Socialism is, in essence, fighting our Founding Fathers. So, if success is truly our guide, if history is doomed to repeat itself, then, using Einstein's definition of insanity, we must be insane to move in this direction. Unfortunately for our children, this is precisely what we are doing.

So what's the most obvious difference between America today and yesterday? It's the same Declaration of Independence, the same Constitution, the same geography, the same melting pot. What have we added or subtracted from the ideological formula that made America exceptional? What motivates man to sacrifice for rather than forsake his fellow citizen? As we move toward secularism, the glaring difference between today and the past is the influence of the 2,000-year-old Christianity in society. Since the majority of Americans still identify as Christian, the answer to our stagnation is for that majority to stand up, unite, and defend those Christian values that were critical components to our greatness.

I've talked to a number of people who see the same thing, public eagerness, after a person has received notoriety, to hear some humiliating news about them. And even worse, it seems that those delivering the news are anxious to tell it even before it has been corroborated. This "guilty until proven innocent" mentality has always been rejected because of the power it gives to deliberate false allegations. And, from a Christian perspective, it seems obvious we should want the accusation to be proven so we do not hurt someone's reputation or have some injustice done to them. However, we watch the achiever being brought down to earth instead of calling out the false accusation. The reporter does not feel any obligation to bury the story until it is confirmed, nor do readers reject the story until it is proven. I look at the "circus" that surrounded Justice Brett Kavanaugh and think of some of America's famous achievers like Thomas Edison or Henry Ford. How would things be different if they were surrounded by uncorroborated allegations? A Christian society should and would want the truth and when society is no longer interested in the truth, we are all in danger . . . and we are certainly not Christian.

America's Christian foundations allow us to recognize not just our rights, but our own duties and responsibilities. Thomas Paine asked Benjamin Franklin to comment on his treatise, *The Age of Reason*. Paine believed man can discern the advantages of virtue and the disadvantages of vice. But, in his response, Franklin defends our religious roots:

> Dear Sir—I have read your manuscript with some attention . . . without the belief of a Providence that takes cognizance of, guards and guides, and may favor particular persons, there is no motive to worship a deity, to fear its displeasure, or to pray for its protection . . .
>
> You yourself may find it easy to live a virtuous life without the assistance afforded by religion—with your having a clear perception of the advantages of virtue and the disadvantages of vice . . . But think how great a portion of mankind have need of the motives of religion to restrain them from vice, support their virtue, and retain them in the practice of it till it becomes habitual . . . And perhaps you are indebted to her originally, that is, to your religious education, for the habits of virtue upon which you now justly value yourself . . .
>
> I would advise you, therefore, not to attempt unchaining the tiger, but to burn this piece before it is seen by any other person . . . If men are so wicked with religion, what would they be without it? . . .
>
> Yours, B. Franklin[2]

Mr. Franklin's response clarifies several of the prevailing components of American thought at that time. Both Franklin and Paine believed that the virtuous life defined by Christian morality is beneficial to a society. However, Benjamin Franklin believed virtue was strengthened by religion and likens its removal to "unchaining the tiger." Also, by advising Paine to "Burn this piece before it is seen by any other person" because of "the enemies it may raise . . . " he is warning him of the predominant loyalty of Americans to the Christian religion. Franklin obviously believes the colonies were religious enough to be angered by disregard for Christianity. And this distinguishes them from the present generation, which expends little effort defending Christianity from the politically correct assault on its traditions.

Human beings do not change their nature over time. The same virtues and vices constantly push us in conflicting ways. It seems, to use Dr. Franklin's expression, that we have "unchained the tiger." The opponents to Christianity certainly do not need to fear confrontation like they did in the time of Franklin and Paine, and so the traditions and institutions that have defined American life since the beginning are now under attack. Traditional marriage, motherhood, and family have been transformed by a modern secularism at odds with traditional Christian teaching. America began as a Christian culture affirming all men are created equal, and thus you would think American culture would be less concerned with diversity and more concerned with what we all have in common, the original design of the family by that same Creator at the moment of Creation.[3] But it is a diversity that is highlighted, causing friction rather than unity.

Since it is man's nature to want to know what is true, what is this modern trend away from absolute truth and instead toward relative truth, especially in a majority Christian country? In Revelation it says, "Because you are lukewarm . . . I will begin to vomit thee out of my mouth." (Revelation 3:16) Is this what is happening then? What distinguishes us is being stripped from us. Today's America is not the America envisioned by Paine, who sought to supplant religion with reason. It is the unchained tiger Franklin warned about that has abandoned not just religion but also morality.

I was discussing American Exceptionalism with a professor from Oregon. He asked what I saw as the main reason the country was struggling to stay on top. I told him there is a crisis of truth. He said, "I agree, look at us for example . . . I'm black, you're white. I'm an only child and you have four brothers. I come from the West Coast and you come from the East Coast. Naturally, with so much different in our lives, we're going to see truth differently." I said, "No, you don't get it at all. The truth does not depend on what you think it is; the truth doesn't depend on what I think it is. It simply 'is' and if we want to be educators, we have to first discover the truth."

'Truth' is not an opinion. This fundamental change to a relative truth is nothing more than a rebellion against any ideological constraints to behavior and is the enemy to human exceptionalism. If all truth is relative, we are freed from any definition of truth that contradicts our personal interpretation and are less motivated to practice the self-control that is necessary for personal sacrifice. Further, relative truth disconnects us from our founding principle, that God is the Creator and, in the process, pushes the culture into the hands of evil. Discipline strengthens a culture, and it is not indulgence but religion that has always guided mankind toward self-discipline.

"Strong minds produce heroes, reject servitude, accept only freedom."[4]

— F. A. Hayek

To enjoy the same success we had in the past, America will need to acknowledge the role Christianity played in that success which is declared by the Founding Fathers themselves.

"Let us humbly commit our righteous cause to the great Lord of the Universe, who loveth righteousness and hateth iniquity . . . let us joyfully leave our concerns in the hands of him who raiseth up and putteth down the empires and kingdoms of the earth as he pleaseth . . . [5] (John Hancock)

Hancock, in the quote above, also implies that every honest effort should be dedicated to God. Then the outcome of our work becomes less important than the effort we put in because the outcome belongs to God.

Expanding the quote of his referenced earlier (on page 153), Elbridge Gerry, signer of the Declaration of Independence and vice president under James Madison, expresses the importance of our service to our country:

"History can hardly produce such a series of events as is taken place in favor of American opposition. The hand of heaven seems to have directed every occurrence. It is the duty of every citizen, though he had but one day to live, to devote that day to the service of his country."[6]

Many years later, addressing the Senate in 1814, Gerry also said: "May that Omnipotent Being, who with infinite wisdom and justice presides over the destinies of nations, confirm the heroic patriotism which is glowed in the breasts of the national rulers and convince the enemy that whilst a disposition to peace on honorable and equitable terms will ever prevail in their public councils, one spirit, animated by the love of country, will inspire every department of the national government."[7]

The national government is given the responsibility of protecting our liberty. However, since 9/11, our priorities have changed. Security now is talked about far more than freedom, but security is worthless if it is purchased at the expense of freedom.

A free society is characterized by the ability to exercise free choice. Why was the Bill of Rights added to the Constitution, and why was protecting the free exercise of religion the first priority for the founders in the Bill of Rights? The Bill of Rights restrains our government and the First Amendment ensures that the people will always be cognizant of true authority over them. "The fear of the Lord is the beginning of wisdom . . . " (Proverbs 9:10). Contrast "fear of the Lord" with fear of your fellow man. The more we trust God, the less we fear man because we know man has no power over eternal life.

I think we need to be skeptical when fear is injected into politics. Politicians like to create the anxiety and then sell you the solution. You have to beware of the politician who promises to give you something to get your vote. After all, who pays for what they promise you? When there is a need, entrepreneurs see it and fill it so as to make a profit and feed their families. Today, fear is created at the threat of cutting a government program because people do not trust that it will be replaced and filled by private citizens. But how can we be a 'United' States if we do not trust each other, if we cannot trust our fellow American? After all, our government is nothing more than just a collection of our fellow Americans.

The late Romanian pastor, Richard Wurmbrand, in his book, *Tortured for Christ*, describes the incredible tortures he and many others received behind the Iron Curtain at the hands of the Communists simply for being Christian. He describes a prisoner named Matchevici, just eighteen years old, at the Tirgu-Ocna prison, severely tortured and very sick with tuberculosis. His family, upon discovering his grave condition, sent him one hundred bottles of streptomycin. The prison officer would not give him the medicine unless he gave up information against his fellow prisoners. He tells us Matchevici's answer:

"I don't wish to remain alive and be ashamed to look in a mirror, because I will see the face of a traitor. I cannot accept such a condition. I prefer to die."[8]

In his example, you see the face of a hero. He not only stood as a witness to what is true and right and good but also protected those who would have been tortured and killed as a result of his answer. Pastor Wurmbrand says:

"One great lesson arose from all the beatings, tortures, and butchery of the Communists: that the spirit is master of the body. We felt the torture, but it often seemed as something distant and far removed from the spirit, which was lost in the glory of Christ in His presence with us."[9]

Richard Wurmbrand has done us a great favor by memorializing this conflict between the Christians and the Communists behind the Iron Curtain. The Communists were atheists. They made themselves God, and therefore, their natural enemy was Christianity. Christians oppose Communism with a ruler who is indestructible. The Communists, while they can conquer the 'body,' cannot conquer the soul and thus can never be secure.

The appeal of Socialism and Communism is the security that no individual will be left behind, stepped on, or forgotten by the powerful and more fortunate. In reality, it is precisely the latter that exercises the authority that keeps the masses where they are. As F. A. Hayek noted:

"I am certain that nothing has done so much to destroy the juridical safeguards of individual freedom as the striving after this mirage of social justice."[10]

When the state replaces God, humans are reduced to mere animals where only the physical matters, as exemplified in Hitler's master race. Christianity, by contrast, teaches the strong to support the weak. By practicing the art of compassion, we learn to sacrifice for the sake of our neighbor. This doesn't just strengthen us by means of endurance and perseverance; it fosters strong communities because of each other's commitment to one another. And strong communities collectively make a strong nation.

Many of the trappings that led to the expansion of Communism and its contempt for human dignity are repeating themselves today. Political debates whip up class envy with charges of growing income disparity between rich and poor, and candidates look to gather a following by promising free healthcare and free tuition. And the reality is this: Not only is nothing free, but the cost of these 'free' things is not just paid for with money. If we depend on another for the things we want, we lose our independence and, as such, we give up a portion of our freedom.

It is no surprise that, at the same pace that we move to Communist thought, we also move away from Christian thought since they are diametrically opposed. It (Communism) is not just a disregard for Christian values; it is hatred for Christianity and hatred of Christ who has the authority they desire. This is the classic battle—Communism versus Christianity, good versus evil, God versus Satan—that is beginning to manifest itself as real persecution.

As we speak, Christians are being murdered in every corner of the world, including here in America. But, while you will always have individuals who will act on their hate, as a nation, we subscribe to the concept of religious liberty. So, what is more alarming is witnessing the unprecedented encroachment into our personal religious convictions. The H.H.S. (Health and Human Services) mandate in Obamacare requiring employers to include contraceptives, abortifacients, and sterilization in their insurance plans even when they conflict with their personal religious beliefs, is taking us backward to the tyranny of the past. Yet, the very same weapon useful for fighting back against this tyranny is always at our fingertips and can never be taken away—the human spirit that finds its origin in God. And if America turns back to her Christian roots, you might find new writers following in the footsteps of Alexis De Tocqueville to describe the modern resurgence of America.

". . . For God did not give us a spirit of cowardice but rather a spirit of power and of love and self-discipline."
— **2 Timothy 1:6-7**

*   *   *

Secularism and Tyranny

"That vice and irreligion may be banished, and Virtue and piety established by grace . . . That the nation may be made a holy nation, and that the religion of our Divine Redeemer, with all its benign influences, may cover the earth as the waters do the sea."[11]
— **The state papers of the Continental Congress**

A government and a people that embrace secularism cannot remain free for long. The spirit of charity begins to disappear. It is no longer exercised regularly because it is no longer relevant; it no longer makes sense. Charity is made clear in Christianity: Love your neighbor as yourself. But in the world without God, our goal is survival. Without morality absolutely defined in the Judeo-Christian tradition, it (charity) becomes subject to moral relativism. Moral relativism leaves the truth of our freedom an ever-changing concept and the Constitution re-interpreted to defend popular passions. Without Christian tradition, all that's really left is improving your position and securing your own welfare; in which case, those best able to secure their own welfare are the strong. In a purely secular world, we naturally move in the direction of tyranny—the epitome of a 'dog-eat-dog world.' Survival of the fittest replaces sacrifice in that we see ourselves as top priority for protection and survival. And that is the best-case scenario. In the worst case, human beings' unbridled lust for power leads the strong to exploit the weak. The Christian founding of America replaced the king with God as ruler. Without God, the power-hungry once again fight for that position.

I think most of us will agree that heroism comes from something born inside a person. Before we begin to examine any kind of religious beliefs or revelation, we must acknowledge our own spiritual self, the deep contemplative part of us that no one else knows or can know. If a society eliminates the concept of the spiritual, it forfeits real purpose, and life is reduced to, simply, the best survival plan. This highly individualistic, egotistic plan cannot serve our society well because we do not all share all the talents visible in humanity. Brilliant minds in art, science, math, language, etc., enhance society and themselves only when their results are shared. The organism that is mankind consists of many talents just like the body has many parts that are intended to work in conjunction with each other. It is very similar to the analogies of the great Saint Paul, who said:

"For as in one body we have many members, but all the members have not the same office; so we, being many, are one body in Christ, and every one, members one of another." (Romans 12:4–5)

This analogy of humanity and its talents with the body and its parts, just like Saint Paul's teaching concerning the Church, offers a portrait of human freedom in that those talents would be rendered useless if people were prevented from using them. But they expose another fact: We have been given our talents by a divine Providence to be used for the other members of the body and therefore are not free to ignore our talents. Instead, we are free to perfect and be excellent at what we are designed for.

The parable of the talents emphasizes our duties in life:

" . . . A man going on a journey called his servants and entrusted to them his property; to one he gave five talents, to another two, to another one; to each according to his ability . . . He who had received the five talents . . . traded with them . . . and he made five talents more. So also, he who had the two talents made two talents more. But he who had received the one talent went and dug in the ground and hid his master's money. Now after a long time the master of those servants came and settled accounts with them. And he who had received the five talents came forward, bringing five talents more . . . His master said to him, 'Well done, good and faithful servant; you have been faithful over a little, I will set thee over much. Enter into the joy of your master.' And he also who had the two talents came forward saying, 'Master, you delivered to me two talents, here I have made two talents more.' His master said to him, 'Well done, good and faithful servant; you have been faithful over a little, I will set you over much. Enter into the joy of your master.' He also who had received the one talent, came forward saying, 'Master, I knew you to be a hard man . . . so I was afraid, and I went and hid your talent in the ground. Here you have what is yours.' But his master answered him, 'You wicked and slothful servant . . . take the talent from him, and give it to him who has the ten talents . . . and cast the worthless servant into the outer darkness.' " (Matthew 25:14–30)

14

EXCEPTIONALISM IS EXCELLENCE

F AITH IN GOD GIVES OUR LABOR MEANING. It changes our focus because faith is less concerned with measuring our success than it is with measuring our effort. Meditating on the catalysts that inspire a person to excellence or accepted mediocrity, two things must be examined—hope and despair. Both depend on the degree a person believes he can change his life and make it better. This exposes one of the subtle evils of Socialism. It deprives men and women of their own vision of achievement, replacing it with the government's vision toward which all must work. The motivation of personal goals collectively responsible for America's greatness is replaced with workers serving a centralized power.

Saint Thomas Aquinas developed the idea of 'freedom for excellence,' a uniquely human capacity that distinguishes humanity from all other creations. There is no other creature in all creation that can recognize and strive for excellence, whose actions can be qualified. In recognizing the achievements of others, we begin to desire achievement and strive for excellence. The achievers raise the bar for everyone. I can remember watching a friend receive an academic award during

189

my grammar school graduation and thinking how I wished I had won the award. Yet, mediocrity that is rewarded can produce negative results even more effectively because mediocrity can be 'achieved' by anyone.

Belgian moral theologian Servais Pinckaers, writing on "freedom for excellence," connects our work ethic to our freedom by arguing achievement, which is desirable, is not possible without work.

"In the beginning the child, despite a desire to learn, will often feel the lessons and exercises as a constraint imposed on freedom and the attractions of the moment . . . But with effort and perseverance, the gifted child will soon make notable progress and will come to play with accuracy and good rhythm, and with a certain ease . . . Soon the child is no longer satisfied with the assigned exercises but will delight in improvising. In this way, playing becomes more personal. The child who is truly gifted and able to keep up these musical studies may become an artist . . . delighting all who hear . . . "[1]

The banging of the keys that may be confused as freedom is a self-imposed constraint on freedom, limiting what is possible. Pinckaers describes a new and limitless freedom, "freedom for excellence," that accomplishes the revealing of a person's unique talent.

"Of course, anyone is free to bang out notes haphazardly on the piano, as the fancy strikes him . . . On the other hand, the person who really possesses the art of playing the piano has acquired a new freedom. He can play whatever he chooses, and also compose new pieces."[2]

This example demonstrates the freeing nature of the pursuit of excellence. The reliance we have on instruction, demonstration, and example to achieve that excellence is also implied here. We depend on models to point us in the direction of excellence. That's why America's famous historical figures set the standard for future greatness.

* * *

Freedom and Hope

As human beings we are inherently free, but does that freedom imply a freedom to behave in a manner that is not human? That would be the polar opposite of anything heroic. To give up life's struggle is despair; it results in falling into temptation and abandoning the struggle for virtue. Anarchy finds a following in despair because it is easier to destroy than it is to build.

It is 'small' heroism that will be found among a prosperous people. It is in plain view when we see them embrace daily drudgery, seeking the ultimate goal of mastery of one's work. Our weakness tempts us to run from life's burdens, while Christianity teaches us to carry our cross in the spirit of Jesus himself.

America's strength has always been the strong protecting the weak. Heroism is not a reflection of physical strength; it is a reflection of a person's spirit. Heroism is nurtured by our Creator and hope for our eternity. It lives in freedom because it is, first and foremost, a choice to be charitable and it dies in the hopelessness of subjugation. Richard Wurmbrand, in *Tortured for Christ*, describes a meeting he had with a Russian prisoner of the Nazis.

"I asked him if he believed in God. If he had said no, I would not have minded it much. It is the choice of every man to believe or disbelieve. But when I asked him this, he lifted his eyes toward me without understanding and said, 'I have no such military order "believe" ' . . . Here stood before me a man whose mind was dead, a man who had lost a great gift God has given to mankind, his individuality."[3]

Heroism can be snuffed out in just the same way when we lose freedom and the hope that we will ever be in control of our own destiny. At the same time, this is the reason why Christianity is seen as a threat to tyrants. The tyrant knows Christians put a different ruler first (God) who they freely choose to serve. He also is threatened by the fact that his power is limited by the belief that freedom cannot be taken away even with the threat of death because Christians wait in anticipation of the next life. Further, no earthly power can exercise authority over their Creator. That is why the Communists tortured Christians behind the Iron Curtain and why Christianity will continue to be the target of evil in the future.

"Nothing is as democratic as death, for all of a sudden, there is no distinction between Jew or Greek, male or female, Socialist or Totalitarian, Republican or Democrat."
- Fulton Sheen

We generally attribute wisdom to age and experience. Some of the wisdom that comes from living life is due to a specific kind of experience. The older we get, the more familiar we become with death. Beginning with grandparents, then relatives, and, as time goes on, friends, co-workers and neighbors; the inevitability of death, even though obvious, becomes more real as we get older and, in the process, many lessons are taught. Archbishop Fulton Sheen's comments on the assassination of President John F. Kennedy drive home the cold reality that every person born shares with every other.

"Nothing is as democratic as death, for all of a sudden, there is no distinction between Jew or Greek, male or female, Socialist or Totalitarian, Republican or Democrat. All suddenly realize the *wickedness* of the world in which we live. Not until we see what is done to the humanity-loving do we grasp the *frenzied hate* which will not be stilled by the tears of a little John or the whimpering sadness of a Caroline . . . It takes sacrificial death to break down the walls of division."[4]

He exposes something that, as we discuss freedom and exceptionalism, is very important. Do we cherish wisdom? If we do, we would be always mindful of the opinions of those who have been around awhile. The very real experience of death slaps us in the face as Bishop Sheen describes in the assassination of President Kennedy. But the young don't share that experience and as such are idealists with limited experience in what can go wrong in life. Yet today, the 'mature' members of our society have ceded their influence to younger, more impressionable leadership and, in the process, we may not see the 'big picture.' Bishop Sheen removes the 'cloak' of labels like Republican and Democrat, revealing a naked wounded humanity that has to endure "wickedness" and "frenzied hate." It points to the very real existence of evil that must be recognized if the free society is to be defended. In the end there are no labels, just God, and the evil in the world loses its power the closer we get to Him. This is the strength the Founding Fathers had and gave to America.

* * *

Socialism—Afraid of Freedom

"I cannot undertake to lay my finger on that article of the Constitution which granted a right to Congress of expending, on objects of benevolence, the money of their constituents."[5]
—James Madison

What is the proper use of government for a free people? Early Americans had very little use for government. When

Americans perceived a need, citizens groups were formed to assist individuals. It is also important to point out that this does not require a consensus or 100 percent participation. That is the reason why free associations of citizens are so effective and efficient—the association does not need to wait for a consensus vote. This not only embraces the Christian principle of charity but also is one factor identified by Alexis De Tocqueville in explaining America's rise to prosperity.

"Wherever there is a new undertaking, at the head of which you would expect to see in France the government and in England some great lord, in the United States you are sure to find an association . . . In America I came across types of associations which I confess I had no idea existed, and I frequently admired the boundless skill of Americans in setting large numbers of people a common goal and inducing them to strive toward that goal voluntarily."[6]

* * *

Subsidiarity and Creativity

Alexis De Tocqueville recognized in early America something not present in England or France. Citizens here instinctively knew that they could take an idea to improve something, convince neighbors, and create a coalition to implement the idea. This is a healthy reflection and implementation of the freedom won by the thirteen colonies. If a community has the ability and successfully solves its problems, it demonstrates the overall strength of the community. The system of 'subsidiarity' properly uses the people and resources closest to the problem first, graduating to larger associations and institutions (including government) when asked for help, who only remain until the problem is solved. The proper role of government is to protect liberty and to allow affected associations the ability to address their own needs whenever and wherever possible. This is what De Tocqueville discovered in practice in America. The definition of subsidiarity below gives true healthy boundaries for and defines the proper role of government.

"Excessive intervention by the state can threaten personal freedom and initiative . . . A community of a higher order should not interfere in the internal life of a community of a lower order, depriving the latter of its functions, but rather should support it in case of need . . . It sets limits for state intervention. It aims at harmonizing the relationships between individuals and societies . . . Widespread participation in voluntary associations and institutions is to be encouraged. In accordance with the principle of subsidiarity, neither the state nor any larger society should substitute itself for the initiative and responsibility of individuals and intermediary bodies."[7]

Socialism is the antithesis of freedom, heroism, and American Exceptionalism because its appeal is generated out of our fears, promising our security and safety, ultimately at the expense of our liberty. Freedom, in contrast, involves maturely facing the uncertainty of life with all of its hardships and enduring. This is the first baby step of heroic accomplishment. De Tocqueville continues:

"The free institutions that Americans possess . . . are, in a thousand ways, constant reminders to each and every citizen that he lives in society. They keep his mind steadily focused on the idea that it is man's duty as well as his interest to make himself useful to his fellow man."[8]

American Exceptionalism begins with individual exceptionalism. Christianity subtly delivers that message especially in the Gospel story where Jesus encounters a rich man who asks how to get to heaven. He tells the rich young man to sell all his belongings and give the proceeds to the poor. Yet, was Christ's objective to make the young man poor or, instead, to help the young man discover something deeper about his own value as a man?

"And behold, one came up to him, saying, Teacher, what good deed must I do, to have eternal life?' And He said to him ' . . . If you would enter life, keep the commandments.' The man said to him, '. . . All these I have observed; what do I still lack?' Jesus said to him, 'If you would be perfect, go, sell what you possess, and give to the poor, and you will have treasure in heaven: and come, follow me.' When the young man heard this, he went away sorrowful: for he had great possessions." (Matthew 19:16–22)

It was precisely because this man was exceptional that Jesus asked this of him, and the objective was to make him more so with "treasure in heaven." He obviously had the talent to make a fortune before and can surely again. As was pointed out in the parable of the talents[9] earlier, every one of us is expected to use the talents given to him by God. Thus, if this man, after giving away his wealth, continues to use the talents that helped him produce his wealth, he will produce more wealth that he can continue to share. And there is no reason anyone cannot do the same with what they've been given in an endless cycle of production and giving. This is the mindset encouraged by Christianity. Moreover, the secret of this parable may be Jesus telling him, "sell what you possess." If we see everything we have as belonging to God, then we possess nothing. In America today, so-called rags-to-riches stories are part of our history and are the American dream. And the more people practice this Christian teaching, the more each person would benefit from the talent of his neighbor, and the more exceptional America would become.

If there were such a thing as a Marxist bible, it might say that the encounter between Jesus and the rich man might continue with Jesus ordering the Apostles to run and tackle the young man, take his belongings by force and sell them, giving the proceeds to the poor people in Jerusalem. Wouldn't that produce a net gain for society? Isn't the common good being achieved when we take the rich man's possessions? There obviously is no Marxist bible, but that perfectly describes where we are today. Empowering an outside authority leaves neither rich nor poor in control of his destiny. If the authority were to abuse its power, they would both become victims. If this rich man will not give to the poor, it is possible the next one will, but when he relinquishes power over his goods, he makes himself permanently vulnerable to those to whom he has given it.

Thus, in a subtle way, the truth of the Christian Gospel also confirms something very American—the right to be secure in our possessions. The modern economics that dominates political debate today should be subservient to this fundamental right. For a nation's wealth to be pooled for any reason, whether by taxation or another method, requires an authority with the power to collect it. The father of our country, George Washington, as well as most Americans of this period, understood clearly that the power to tax also gives the potential to enslave if that power is abused. Personal wealth and property rights are the products of free enterprise and fundamental incentives for a prosperous society.

"I think the Parliament of Great Britain hath no more right to put their hands into my pocket, without my consent, than I have to put my hands into yours for money . . ."[10] (George Washington)

Do we share that vision today? If we fast-forward to our present time, 2016 and 2020 Democratic Party presidential candidate Senator Bernie Sanders has said he is comfortable taxing the wealthy (whoever they are) 90 percent.[11] As I write this, he has continued campaigning for free college tuition, among other things. He justifies this Socialist objective by making education a right rather than a duty while neglecting to mention that public education is not free. Teachers, maintenance engineers, and administrators have not made a secret agreement to work for nothing. Nor have book publishers, stationery retailers, etc. made any such agreement. No, education becomes "free" for Bernie Sanders by diverting more money from other places to finance it, and his proposal is motivated by sheer political ambition. However, his popularity says something about modern America. At no time in our past would we have embraced such a notion.

To better understand what is involved in any Socialist promise, it is important to contemplate why governments want to offer it. In 1891, Pope Leo XIII commented on the moral dangers attached to a diminished value of property rights. Faced with the evil of Socialism, he shed light on what is at risk:

> **"It is no easy matter to define the relative rights and mutual duties of the rich and of the poor, of capital, and of labor. And the danger lies in this, that crafty agitators are intent on making use of these differences of opinion to pervert men's judgments and to stir up the people to revolt . . . They (Socialist contentions) are, moreover, emphatically unjust, for they would rob the lawful possessor, distort the functions of the state and create utter confusion in the community."[12]**

Isn't this exactly what we see happening today? Economic wealth is not moral wealth, and it is moral wealth that is lacking. The politicians who cry out, "The wealthy and the large corporations need to pay their fair share," sound like the 'crafty agitators' that the Pope is speaking of. In America, the government's role is designed to protect the lawful possessor, not to stir up envy over each other's possessions, yet envy is precisely what is being encouraged. Christianity clearly teaches it is our role as individuals to look after our neighbor, and, to the degree we accept this responsibility, we limit the need for government. That is the greatest protection of freedom. This encyclical makes a critical correlation between you and your work, your wages, and your property that suggests that when a government takes a person's wages or property, they have taken their work.

" . . . when a man engages in remunerative labor, the impelling reason and motive of his work is to obtain property . . . he therefore expressly intends to acquire a right, full and real, not only to the remuneration, but also to the disposal of such remuneration, just as he pleases . . . Thus, if he . . . invests his savings in land, the land, in such case, is only his wages under another form; and, consequently, a working man's little estate thus purchased should be as completely at his full disposal as are the wages he receives for his labor . . . Socialists, therefore, by endeavoring to transfer the possessions of individuals to the community at large, strike at the interests of every wage-earner, since they would deprive him of the liberty of disposing of his wages, and thereby of all hope and possibility of increasing his resources and of bettering his condition in life."[13]

A firefighter friend of mine and I used to argue about the need for government in our daily life (and we still do). One day, shortly after Hurricane Sandy devastated New York and

New Jersey, he came up to me and said, "I guess we do need government's help once in a while." I knew what he meant, but playing dumb, I said, "What do you mean?" He said, "Come on, the hurricane!" I continued, "What are you talking about?" He said, "Obviously we need government help, right. You know, like FEMA." I asked him, "How long has FEMA been around?" He said, "I don't know." I told him, "FEMA was created under President Jimmy Carter and has only been around since 1979. What did we do before that—panic?"

The truth is, as every firefighter well knows, that before that we watched the Red Cross respond, which is just one example of an association formed by Americans to satisfy their needs. This is not to suggest there is no place for government at all because, in this example, for instance, the Red Cross may determine their resources to be insufficient for the tragedy and call for additional help. But that help should begin and end with the Red Cross, not the government.

Firefighting often sent me into poverty-stricken areas. I saw people in those moments become completely dependent on firefighters. We essentially became their good neighbors, saving what little property they had. Those victims value their property every bit as much as anyone else and they recognize how irreplaceable any good Samaritan is in those moments.

Individuals, free to pursue their goals and talents, are limited only by themselves. Collectively, their free pursuits help produce a flourishing society by tapping into human ingenuity and a shared desire to succeed. In contrast to this freedom, a slave must be coerced; he will do nothing but what he is told because he has no incentive to do more. Similarly, as Pope Leo pointed out, Socialism denies you the liberty of disposing of your wages and the liberty of bettering your life through your own efforts and according to your own vision.

Worst of all, if government decides how to use your income, they might well decide one day to keep it.

I can remember my grandmother, who raised eleven children through the Great Depression, saying, "I don't need anybody's charity." America's rich heritage of freedom will survive only if America repels fear and envy and endures hardship. In the words of Abraham Lincoln:

> "... Property is the fruit of labor; property is desirable, is a positive good in the world. That some should be rich shows that others may become rich, and hence is just encouragement to industry and enterprise. Let not him who is houseless pull down the house of another, but let him work diligently and build one for himself, thus by example assuring that his own shall be safe from violence when built."[14]

Can living this life on earth ever be 'safe'? As long as people are subject to their own human flaws, permanent, continual safety cannot be achieved. The wealth of one person can and should be used to benefit the underprivileged just as we saw in the Gospel concerning the rich man (Matthew 19:16–22). The real danger is giving a third party (government) what was originally your responsibility. Government then can play the role of 'Robin Hood,' with the power to take wealth from one to give to another . . . and the potential to abuse that power.

There is a subtle message that comes from the words of Jesus: "The poor you will always have with you . . . " (Mark 14:7) There is no revelation from Jesus offering a solution to poverty. He never told anyone, "If everyone would give, no one will be poor," otherwise He would have insisted on it. Ending poverty is not possible without changing humanity itself. The benefit is that, in that way, God ensures there will always be a place for charity in each person's heart because the human condition will always need it. From the Red Cross to groups like 'Feed the Children,' like-minded Americans have united for every cause you can think of. That's why, as I said earlier, Franklin was right about the danger of trading liberty for safety. There is no wisdom in trading what we need for the dream of something we cannot fully obtain.

Socialism is a lie because it masks its true intention—the consolidation of power. It succeeds by encouraging envy in society, dividing instead of uniting, to advance its goals by comparing the amount of property individuals have and promising to equalize it. Equalizing outcomes ignores effort *and* the human talent responsible for varying degrees of productivity with the real effect being loss of freedom and the crushing of initiative because the talented have no more to gain from their efforts than the untalented.

Jesus described the people who would enter heaven as those who gave to the least of their brothers. Similarly, He said He would judge those who, when they saw Him, gave Him no drink, gave Him no food, etc. He does not, however, recommend that those who refuse to give should have their property taken by another so that all things are equal. If we believe Christ, we personally have a duty to our neighbor that cannot be transferred to anyone else, especially the government.

Further, Socialism dilutes property rights, making it difficult to exercise your own charity. Our ability to be charitable necessarily depends upon our personal property rights because we must have something that is definitely ours to give. Charity is not something that is taken. It has to be given. So, when Socialism (today, the welfare state) claims to take care of the common good, the government fills a role which is not their own by taking what is not their own. It nefariously denies the truth that our work and its fruits belong to God and that we share that work with our neighbor who is made in His image.

It is hard to resist the temptation of someone who promises something for nothing. We all feel the burdens of life, and we all occasionally have doubts about our future. Communists appeal to the poor because the poor are overwhelmed by their need and find attractive the promise of equal living standards for everyone. And it is easy to stir up hostility toward the wealthy who do not struggle for a meal. The sin of envy is whipped up in the masses, with the Communists playing God by taking from one and giving to another. This is not an exaggeration but a sad reality. There is no charity in Communism, only despair. The lessons learned throughout the twentieth century are still seen today. In his book, Pastor Wurmbrand describes a conversation, while he was a prisoner in Romania in the 1950s, between a prison guard, Reck, and a prisoner named Grecu, whom Reck was ordered to slowly beat to death: it's a story that illustrates how dehumanization is the real product of this evil.

"You know, I am God. I have power of life and death over you. The one who is in heaven cannot decide to keep human life. Everything depends upon me. If I wish, you live. If I wish, you are killed. I am God!"[15]

The natural progression of Socialism is the denial of human dignity and the distortion of human equality. That is the consequence of unchecked power.

Through humility, we can admit our weaknesses. The Founding Fathers promoted public humility by acknowledging their dependence on God, calling for national days of prayer and fasting, and for days of Thanksgiving. It takes recognizing our flaws to be on our guard. And in order to change, we must deny ourselves those vices because the temptation is to ignore our conscience and satiate ourselves. If human beings are subject to their own flaws, how can they set their own limits? The basis for law has to come from something greater than Man for it to be effective.

Throughout Judeo-Christian tradition, in both the Old and New Testaments, God has revealed both temptation and tempter. In Dante's *Inferno*, Dante Alighieri describes the seven deadly sins.[16] A hard look at the detailed list reminds us that we are all sadly afflicted with these temptations, but also that civilization depends on them being controlled:

1. The first deadly sin is Lust, whereby we entertain obsessive or excessive desires thereby putting God second.

2. Second is Gluttony. It is the overindulgence of anything to the point of waste. The glutton is slave to his animal desires (such as appetite) and in this way is akin to lust. One's gluttony ignores God's generosity and deprives the needy through one's waste.

3. The third deadly sin is Greed. Yet another sin of excess related to the first two, greed is the excessive love of money. The greedy are selfish and uncharitable, choosing perishable treasure over eternal treasure, loving wealth over God.

4. The fourth is Sloth. Characterized today as laziness, it is sadness and apathy coming from our inability to recognize God's gifts. Thus, we fail to love God with all our being. Instead of being an 'excess,'

it is 'absence' of love.

5. Next is Wrath, which is anger or hatred coming from distorting a love of justice into revenge and spite, thereby negating the ability to forgive.

6. Sixth, Envy, Saint Thomas Aquinas calls "sorrow for another's good."

7. Seventh is Pride, the worst sin of all. It led to Lucifer's downfall and manifests itself in us in so many ways. It is the root of all the other sins because it perverts love of self into hatred for your neighbor.

Pride, however, plays a part in nearly every aggression, and we are all victims of it. The sinful nature described by Dante is common to all men and the primary obstacle in our pursuit of excellence, used by the devil specifically for our failure.

The American Declaration of Independence begins as a reflection on the intentions of nature's God for mankind. The self-evident truths highlighted in those opening paragraphs denote his sovereignty. As far as our country is concerned, by beginning with God, that document places all Christian revelation, including the seven deadly sins, in a definitive place. Without God, we become judge of ourselves, beset with the same temptations, passions, and vices.

This brings us back to the work of our own hands and the sharing of our talents. In the Old Testament Book of Genesis, it says that when God was finished creating the heavens and the earth, "He rested on the seventh day from all His work which He had done." (Genesis 2:2) However, the word for work used in the translation does not mean toil. As the scripture passage suggests, to create and to work in those first moments of existence are synonymous. Created in His image and likeness, man is given the example of God at work in the act of creating. The concept of work as a unique expression of an individual's own gifts is supported by the definition of the Hebrew word for work. Hebrew scholar Benno Jacob says:

"The Hebrew word for work is related to the word for messenger and indicates the realization of a thought, desire, and intention. The Creator gave something of himself into his work as a man puts a part of himself into his. . . . The work represents him and speaks of him. Thus, the creation speaks of God. The conception of 'labor', either hard or easy, is not contained in the Hebrew word."[17]

From this point of reference, we can see the reflection of the worker in his work. I was listening to a talk given by a Franciscan Friar of the Renewal. The priest said that, with new facial recognition technology, they can look across the globe and find someone who looks just like you. But, he said, "They are not you." You are unique, you have your own soul. No two people are the same and, without you, the world can never be the same because there is no one else who can add exactly what you would to the world. The priest was commenting on the souls lost to abortion, but the same point can be made concerning Socialism and Communism where their central control takes away individual choice from society. If we deny the person the chance to work in a way that expresses his own unique gifts, it changes the world in much the same way as if they did not exist.

Christ said, "And do not fear those who kill the body but cannot kill the soul; rather fear him who can destroy both soul and body in hell." (Matthew 10:28)

Living in America does not remove the threats to our liberty. Courage comes with faith, and we are living in a post-9/11 society extraordinarily concerned with its safety. I think we need to be skeptical when fear is injected into politics. Politicians seem to be creating anxiety and then selling you the solution. Everything comes with a price tag, and we cannot afford to pay for it with our liberty.

15

EXCEPTIONALISM AND THE WORK ETHIC

I CAN'T HELP BUT NOTE IN THE STUDYING OF GEORGE WASH-INGTON'S letters how often he signs them "your most obedient and humble servant." The image of everyone in service to each other makes quite a powerful statement, especially coming from our first president. Words like these from prominent powerful figures always capture my attention. I look at George Washington as anything but obedient and humble; however, that is how he wants to be seen to the reader.

Without a doubt, the combined efforts of individuals have greater impact than the singular efforts of one person. Washington's service to his nation, when we consider his stature, resembles this part of the Gospel of Matthew, where Jesus says:

" . . . Whoever would be great among you must be your servant, and whoever would be first among you must be your slave; even as the Son of Man came not to be served but to serve, and to give his life as a ransom for many." (Matthew 20:26–28)

The collective action of people in service to one another is demonstrated on the military battlefield. Commanders always seek to have a fighting force larger than the enemy—the more overwhelming the better. When I was a firefighter, it was common for chiefs to call for more manpower when it was deemed necessary. As he assessed increased need at the emergency, the chief would increase the response from "All Hands" to "Second Alarm," "Third Alarm," etc., until the fire was under control. Everybody there was committed to extinguishing the fire and removing victims, and that commitment resulted in success. But that success would quickly evaporate if the firefighters were not committed to each other.

The success of Washington is undeniable. The traits he thought necessary to achieve success in life came from a self-imposed discipline that he wished his army to embody. He makes this clear in his general orders:

"It is required and expected that exact discipline be observed, and due subordination prevail thro' the whole army, as a failure in these most essential points must necessarily produce extreme hazard, disorder and confusion; and end in shameful disappointment and disgrace."[1]

The same way that heroes provide a model of achievement, General Washington connects our honorable self-discipline to success on the battlefield, but its practice can benefit achievement in everyday life. He also saw the importance of sobriety and reverence to God to augment that self-discipline:

"The general most earnestly requires, and expects, a due observance of those articles of war, established for the government of the Army, which forbid profane cursing, swearing, and drunkenness; and in like manner requires and expects, of all officers, and soldiers, not engaged on actual duty, a punctual attendance on divine service, to implore the blessings of heaven upon the means used for our safety and defense."[2]

From the time I was a young boy, George Washington, for me, has always ranked first as an American hero, a model for our own patriotism. The America he guided produced the fruits of exceptionalism. If we go by the earlier premise that heroes must sacrifice for something greater than themselves, then Washington becomes the most obvious example. His actions are led by a goal outside of his personal life—American independence. And his deeds are colored by a quality that he most respects—virtue. In his own words:

"The cause of America and of liberty is the cause of every virtuous American citizen whatever may be his religion or his descent, the united colonies know no distinction, but such as slavery, corruption, and arbitrary domination may create. Come then, ye generous citizens, raise yourselves under the standard of general liberty, against which all the force in artifice of tyranny will never be able to prevail."[3]

The Bible's first lesson on virtue comes in its very first pages when it provides the example of a Creator engaged in productive work.

"Thus the heavens and the earth and all their array were completed. Since on the seventh day God was finished with the work he had been doing, he rested on the seventh day from all the work he had undertaken." (Genesis 2:1–2)

Work is first revealed in the 'objects' produced by the ultimate 'craftsman,' God, and it is God who makes clear to us that the things he created are "very good."[4] And these objects of his work come forth from his divine imagination. Naturally, since God is perfect, his work reveals work in its perfection. Therefore, since Man himself is created in his image, the pinnacle of creation, it logically follows that we would reflect Him in all things—including his original work of Creation. By using the resources of the Earth in conjunction with our

211

individual imaginations and talents, we fulfill our destiny by working in the "image and likeness of God."

"God created man in His image; in the divine image He created him; male and female He created them. God blessed them, saying: 'Be fertile and multiply; fill the earth and subdue it. Have dominion over the fish of the sea, the birds of the air, and all the living things that move on the earth.' " (Genesis 1:27–28)

God expects us to perform good works within our personal capacities. Every individual's 'pursuit of happiness' is expressed in his or her unique personal and individual expression of work, according to talents that are not chosen by him, but instead received as a gift from his Creator. This is good. That original image of creation is propagated time and time again through the work of every person because he emulates God in whose image he is made. Thus, creation, begun at the beginning of time, properly continues throughout all eternity.

"Human work proceeds directly from persons created in the image of God and called to prolong the work of creation by subduing the earth, both with and for one another."[5]

Thus, in the spirit of truth revealed in Judeo-Christian tradition, the work, challenges, and dangers, collectively known as our crosses, inspire our productivity and innovation and improve the world. Today as we drift into secularism, challenges and dangers are converted from crosses into fears. In the face of those challenges, rather than look to the ultimate power and authority of the Creator, men begin to anticipate danger and worry about safety instead of looking for solutions. People, once they succumb to fear, become vulnerable to the tyrant. This is another evil of Socialism: to replace a spiritual understanding of our pain and suffering with one of dependence.

"If an American is to amount to anything, he must rely upon himself, and not upon the State; he must take pride in his own work, instead of sitting idle to envy the luck of others. He must face life with resolute courage, win victory if he can, and accept defeat if he must, without seeking to place on his fellow man a responsibility which is not theirs."[6] (Theodore Roosevelt)

The Socialist mindset robs people of the mature embrace of responsibility, trading it for an authoritarian government that speaks like a parent to his children. While Christ asks us to carry our cross, Socialism encourages us to beg government to remove it. Suffering, unavoidable in this life, is stripped of any meaning or value and its ability to build character is not taken advantage of. Absent the struggle to overcome obstacles, man, just as an unused muscle, atrophies.

"If an American is to amount to anything, he must rely upon himself, and not upon the State; He must take pride in his own work, instead of sitting idle to envy the luck of others."

- Theodore Roosevelt

"We do not admire the man of timid peace. We admire the man who embodies victorious effort; the man who never wrongs his neighbor, who is prompt to help a friend, but who has those virile qualities necessary to win in the stern strife of actual life. It is hard to fail, but it is worse never to have tried to succeed. In this life, we get nothing save by effort."[7]

There is no real freedom that is absent of any need to work. A person, where he is not self-reliant, is dependent. That is when he looks for the help of those closest to him: family, friends, community, etc. The government's job is to protect the freedom of all so that we are able help each other. And, protected and cherished in the Declaration of Independence is the principle that it is our nature to be free:

"When in the course of human events, it becomes necessary for one people to dissolve the political bands which have connected them with another, and to assume among the powers of the earth, the separate and equal station to which the Laws of Nature and of Nature's God entitle them, a decent respect to the opinions of mankind requires that they should declare the causes which impel them to the separation.

"We hold these truths to be self-evident, that all men are created equal, that they are endowed by their Creator with certain unalienable rights, that among these are life, liberty, and the pursuit of happiness . .

"We, therefore, the Representatives of the United States of America, in Gen. Congress, assembled, appealing to the Supreme Judge of the world for the rectitude of our intentions, do, in the name, and by Authority of the good people of these colonies, solemnly publish and declare, that these United colonies are, and of right ought to be free and independent states . . . And for the support of this declaration, with a firm reliance on the protection of Divine Providence, we mutually pledge to each other our Lives, our Fortunes, and our sacred Honor."[8]

Each highlight points to affirmations in the American mind of God's authority over man and that his freedom is part of God's primordial plan. The same America that affirmed God's authority also reaped unprecedented prosperity. We are created subject to God, not man. As both Judaism and Christianity hold that all power, glory, and honor belong to the Creator, the United States of America holds as truth the principle of freedom from tyranny. Rights endowed by God can only be taken by God.

"The operating presupposition is, first, that there is a Creator who, at a point in time, brought into being everything that is. This Creator understands His creation in all its detail."[9] (Michael Novak)

This is in stark contrast to the nations and principalities that came before, where even the Christian nations did not connect their beginnings to defending this presupposition. I heard Dr. Alan Keyes make the point many years ago, and I think he's right that America is exceptional because she is an *exception* to tyranny.

* * *

Teaching Our Children the American Way

Education is more than simply passing on information. It requires moving the young and impressionable toward a love of truth, especially concerning our created nature. Knowledge of history prevents us from repeating the mistakes of the past so that we do not have to learn those lessons the hard way, repeating the same mistakes over and over again. We must pass on the truth to future generations if the America we know and love, the America that protects our right to life, liberty, and the pursuit of happiness, is to survive.

Past statesmen have insisted that, as a people, we must undergird all education with virtue and patriotism as a prerequisite to continued success.

"Every child in America should be acquainted with his own country. He should read books that furnish him with ideas that will be useful to him in life and practice. As soon as he opens his lips, he should rehearse the history of his own country; he

215

should lisp the praise of liberty, and of those illustrious heroes and statesmen, who have wrought a revolution in her favor." [10]
— **Noah Webster, 1788**

"We cannot afford to differ on the question of honesty if we expect our republic permanently to endure. Honesty is not so much a credit as an absolute prerequisite to efficient service to the public. Unless a man is honest, we have no right to keep him in public life; it matters not how brilliant his capacity." [11] (Theodore Roosevelt)

"Patriotism means to stand by the country. It does not mean to stand by the President or any other public official save exactly to the degree in which he himself stands by the country . . . Every man who parrots the cry of 'Stand by the President' without adding the proviso 'so far as he serves the Republic' takes an attitude as essentially unmanly as that of any Stuart royalist who championed the doctrine that the King could do no wrong. No self-respecting and intelligent free man could take such an attitude." [12] (Theodore Roosevelt)

"My fondest hope for each one of you, and especially for the young people here, is that you will love your country, not for her power or wealth, but for her selflessness and her idealism. May each of you have the heart to conceive, the understanding to direct, and the hand to execute works that will make the world a little better for your having been here. May all of you as Americans never forget your heroic origins, never fail to seek divine guidance, and never lose your natural, God-given optimism. And finally, my fellow Americans, may every dawn be a great new beginning for America and every evening bring us closer to that shining city upon a hill." (Ronald Reagan, August 17, 1992 speech to Republican National Convention)

Exceptionalism and the Work Ethic

A proud view of our American history, the fostering of patriotism, and a commitment to truth, are being replaced with harsh criticism, and we must beware of looking so hard for faults and thereby missing the treasure. When it comes to educating our children, Truth is the first priority, more important than proficiency in any subject, and the country's success or failure in the future will depend on whether we have taught a respect for truth.

16

THE PACKAGING

W HEN I WAS AT MANHATTAN COLLEGE STUDYING BUSINESS
ADMINISTRATION, I became interested in, and finally
chose, marketing as my major. I have always been a very social
creature, and marketing was an excellent fit because it focuses
on people and how they think, empathizing with them, learn-
ing from them—all to discover what they react to. In the
course of my studies, I learned that a manufacturer seeking
to market his product must learn what attracts a consumer as
well as dissuades him. Successful market analysis has as much
or more to do with the success of a product as its quality or
price. This is the philosophy of advertising—to know your
customer.

One of the subtopics of advertising is the packaging of
what is being sold. And the first thing that you learn is the
choice of packaging is more about attractiveness than it is
about information. It will employ colors, shapes, sizes, and
images to first, make you look at it and, second, to create a
perception that you need their product. In the long run, the
packaging is successful when you, the consumer, are attracted
to it. The hope is to make you desire the product.

In this way, you can clearly see the role that emotion plays in the success or failure of any promotion. The concept of successful packaging, spoken about in virtually all business circles, is not just for business nor is it applicable to physical goods alone. It can similarly be applied to the agendas of individuals or groups of ambitious persons or parties. Intellectual property, ideas, and debate techniques all employ language to package what they are 'selling.' To really see the goal or agenda, it is necessary to remove the packaging to see what is really underneath. In a discussion about American Exceptionalism and its decline, a thorough analysis requires at least some consideration as to who would gain from American decline.

During the Cold War, the Soviet Union had a definite interest in undermining America's strength. From a marketing perspective, a good way to begin would be to redefine our values, to 're-package' our strengths as weaknesses. As terms like 'globalization' and the 'global economy' become common parlance in the general public, some questions must be answered. Are international trade and removing trade barriers 'globalization'? Political forces are moving the world toward globalization, but from a political perspective, this can only be good if it enhances human freedom and individual liberty.

Hypothetically, in a world of many economic and political systems, if one particular one is actually superior, globalization would have to move the other systems toward it for globalization to be good. If the opposite should happen, then globalization would be harmful. From a purely American point of view, we see politics tearing at our traditions and institutions while simultaneously advancing a global agenda.

American Exceptionalism is being portrayed as an archaic term that no longer is relevant and, in so doing, we Americans are no longer making the founding principles a priority for American survival. But the lessons from the founding run deeper than American survival. The Christian influence, prayers, and acknowledgment of the Creator give the world a path toward human exceptionalism that we have the responsibility of preserving. The fruit the world has received from an exceptional America demands attention to the causes for exceptionalism. Perceptions mean everything, both in elections and policymaking, just as they do in business, and there is an effort to create the perception of mediocrity. We must all actively participate in the defense of freedom, because our freedom is always the end game of those who lust for power. It bears repeating the quote from George Washington:

"They serve to organize faction . . . to put, in the place of the delegated will of the nation the will of a party, often a small but artful and enterprising minority of the community; and . . . to make the public administration the mirror of the ill-concerted and incongruous projects of faction . . . Associations of the above description . . . are likely, in the course of time and things, to become potent engines, by which cunning, ambitious, and unprincipled men will be enabled to subvert the power of the people and to usurp for themselves the reins of government, destroying afterwards the very engines which have lifted them to unjust dominion."[1]

In the January 2015 issue of *Imprimis* from Hillsdale College, Jason L. Riley, an editorial board member of *The Wall Street Journal*, is quoted from his speech at the college. Mr. Riley, a black man, titled his talk "Race Relations and Law Enforcement." He provides a subtle example of 'packaging' as it relates to race relations.

"Obama was doing exactly what the Left has been conditioning blacks to do since the 1960s, which is to blame black pathology on the legacy of slavery and Jim Crow . . . Meanwhile, the civil rights movement has become an industry that does little more than monetize white guilt."

He is pointing out nothing more than an example of how the packaging of the civil rights movement is being used to advance a different agenda. This is the heart of any successful propaganda campaign—the cleverer the packaging, the better the sale. And in our present-day politics, what's for sale is proverbial snake oil. Here, the distortion of the civil rights movement weakens black and white, while enriching a small group of politicians and activists at the expense of both. The only difference between this example and my marketing class is the product. It is no longer the packaging of widgets for sale but, instead, the propaganda of those in power sold to trusting masses without legitimate sources of information.

Another speech provides a second example. President Obama talked about the success ISIS has had recruiting people because we hadn't addressed their "grievances."[2] This is an attempt to shift attention away from ineffective policy concerning ISIS by suggesting America inadvertently instigates their actions. His speech is an attempt to repackage the conflict. Does he really mean that murder is the appropriate response to ignorance? Either way, the argument is irrelevant unless the supposed 'grievance' of ISIS is true. This conclusion is ridiculous and would be impossible to defend unless the terrorists' motives were successfully repackaged in his speech to suggest that we have behaved wrongly. We can't even begin to talk about justice until we first know what is true, and in this case the truth is there is no justification for their evil acts against the innocent. The solution is to remove the packaging to see what is truly underneath. Here we remove the discussion of 'grievances' to find an administration covering for its failing agenda.

Here, it's the truth behind the grievance and not the grievance itself that matters. If the president packages American guilt rather than American Exceptionalism by unjustly contemplating the grievances of ISIS after an attack, everyone moves further away from justice. Leadership itself is proving that the American Way is under attack by evil, and that might do more to inspire the next generation of patriotic young people than anything else for what is the unseen war, the war against Truth.

There are many terms currently being used to falsely package ideas. The words *radical* and *extremism* are being attached to groups such as the Tea Party, Republicans, pro-life organizations, and Christians in general, all aimed at creating a perception of irrationality. Other terms like *liberal* and *conservative*, *left* and *right*, are being attached to individuals in order to pigeonhole them into a category. For instance, Evangelical might be described as right-wing, or Democrat as left-wing, so that if I tell you I'm Evangelical, for instance, you now paint me with a broad brush that encompasses every stance associated with radical right-wing beliefs. This false packaging ends any worthwhile debate before it has a chance to begin simply by demonizing opposing viewpoints. It causes so many to overreact emotionally rather than reflect thoroughly on our disputes. By falling prey to that tactic, we move rapidly toward fascism. As discussion on politics becomes merely a power struggle.

*　*　*

Exceptionalism and Our Revolution

The founding of America was possible only because of the collective heroism of the American colonists. Their deep belief that freedom came from God made any compromise of liberty impossible and any sacrifice, including their life, justified. When we look at our greatest American hero, George Washington, he rises above the other patriots of that era because power did not corrupt him. He was so esteemed by his fellow officers, patriots, and the rest of the colonists that he could have, with no effort, given himself absolute power.

Yet, obvious as this was to him, he was not motivated for his own personal exaltation. In fact, it was quite the opposite. He loathed the public spotlight and had to be begged to seek the presidency for both the first and the second terms. Washington was, however, a man who shared a vision with other men, for a country where people could pursue their own path in freedom and unity with their countrymen and not coerced by authority. He was committed to lead these fellow countrymen toward this goal, regardless of the outcome. For all of them, the way one lives mattered more than just living. That's why Patrick Henry said, " . . . Give me liberty or give me death," because life is only meant to be lived one way—free.

In the early years of our country, newfound freedom paired with a distinct Christian mindset, which I have demonstrated throughout this book, unleashed the broad scope of talent that human beings possess, and the country realized unbridled success. The people's individual goals and accomplishments were the nation's because the goals of a nation and its people were one and the same. Every personal success was a national success. Just as the dreams of the pioneers were realized, so were the country's dreams of westward expansion. We applauded the discoveries of our countrymen and connected our country's founding to the enabling of our citizens.

Just as by adding Christian thought we achieved success, by removing it we see decline. The modern-day move toward secularism is proving destructive to us as a nation because, untethered from Christianity and the larger goal of national success, our motivation is self-centered. This is the result of radical individualism, democracy without the unifying power of a shared belief system. This individualism you can see manifested in the value given to diversity and the importance given to being a melting pot without explaining why. The idea of equality in democratic societies without the lens of the Christian religion gives greater importance to physical equality of outcomes and less to individual liberty; hence today the cries are of a widening gap between rich and poor without a similar angst over the loss of subtle freedoms. Shared religious belief in a society is unifying; individualism without it is dividing. Alexis De Tocqueville makes this observation about equality:

> "It must be acknowledged that equality . . . suggests to men some very dangerous propensities. It tends to isolate them from one another, to concentrate every man's attention upon himself; and lays open the soul to an inordinate love of material gratification.

> "The greatest advantage of religion is to inspire diametrically contrary principles. There is no religion that does not place the object of man's desires above and beyond the treasures of the earth and that does not naturally raise his soul to regions far above those of the senses. Nor is there any which does not impose on man some duties toward his kind and thus draw him at times from the contemplation of himself."[3]

If our prosperity was the direct result of the founders' faith, then the only way to return to prosperity is through "old-fashioned repentance," and for us to return to offering our life to the God who gave it to us. This was the sentiment expressed by the men responsible for the American Revolution. They act as my teachers because they express these ideas unanimously and have left their writings for me to learn from. It took strong people to found this country, and it will take strong people to return it to prosperity. We have to be what we have always been—the America where the strong protect the weak—not an America where the strong use the weak. And how can we be that in America if we don't collectively believe that we ultimately answer to God? How can we expect his blessings while stating he has no place in our governance?

"Sir, we are not weak, if we make a proper use of those means which the God of nature has placed in our power."
- **Patrick Henry**

" . . . Sir, we are not weak, if we make a proper use of those means which the God of nature has placed in our power. Three millions of people, armed in the holy cause of liberty, and in such a country as that which we possess, are invincible by any force which our enemy can send against us . . . The battle, sir, is not to the strong alone; it is to the vigilant, the active, the brave . . . Is life so dear, or peace so sweet, as to be purchased at the price of chains and slavery? Forbid it, Almighty God! . . . "[4] (Patrick Henry)

Faith prevailed then, but that same faith is needed again today.

* * *

Freedom vs. Power

"On every question of construction, let us carry ourselves back to the time when the Constitution was adopted, recollect the spirit manifested in the debates, and instead of trying what meaning may be squeezed out of the text, or invented against it, conform to the probable one in which it was passed."[5] (Thomas Jefferson)

For the purpose of this comparison, this quote by Thomas Jefferson, spoken nearly fifty years after the signing of the Declaration of Independence, is a perfect place to begin. Now, almost 230 years since the ratification of our Constitution, what he warned against is happening. As I have said, to repeat actions that have historically failed expecting a different result is insane. Here, instead, we compare one people's success with another people's failures. But to do so, we must be on the same page. The founders were successful not because they discovered the solution to every individual's problems but because they ensured that we breathed the fresh air of freedom. This is the true role of government. If we look to government to solve all our problems, we weaken ourselves. And it is more than just a question of freedom versus security, but one of power given away which will not return except by force. Every bit of the power we hand over to elected representatives is forever gone.

How many Americans have never read the Declaration of Independence and the Constitution of the United States of America? How many schools demand it be taught to our children? If the answer is less than all, we are in danger of repeating the history of the republics that have disappeared. Maybe it would help if we imagined those documents were written in the blood of Jefferson or Madison. In starting the Revolutionary War, the signers of the Declaration made their own welfare secondary, and their commitment to their posterity is made obvious in the care taken to create our government. Hurdles and hardship, danger and fear, challenge us and actually produce the environment from which greatness emerges. Yet, just as easily as it can produce exceptionalism, hardship, danger, and fear can crush it if fear wins out over courage.

There was a permeating spirit the founders inherited from

the Pilgrims, who had been victims of religious persecution. The Constitution reflects not just a religious spirit, but the Christian spirit. The Founding Fathers recognized government must be composed of its citizens and not a ruling elite. The fact that its citizens are the source of its governing authority is not enough to secure freedom for their posterity because the future will produce potential tyrants of its own. A written Constitution allows the principle to survive only if it recognizes its source is God. Otherwise, human flaws and our own evils will pervert its purpose until it becomes meaningless.

"And can the liberties of a nation be thought secure when we have removed their only firm basis, a conviction in the minds of the people that these liberties are the gift of God? That they are not to be violated but with his wrath? Indeed, I tremble for my country when I reflect that God is just: that his justice cannot sleep forever . . . "[6] (Thomas Jefferson)

"Our peculiar security is in the possession of a written Constitution. Let us not make it a blank paper by construction." (Thomas Jefferson to W. Nicholas, 1803)[7]

* * *

Modern Myths

I have been talking about this topic for quite some time now. One day at work, a coworker named Pete came up, generously offering to me a book he had just read. He said, "Frank, I think you'll like this book. It explains how the Founding Fathers were really not Christians at all. They were actually deists." Challenging the point, I asked him a question, "Do you agree that Christianity is being attacked?" He wasn't sure. So, I asked, "How about in the media? Traditional Christian concepts on marriage that are even shared by other religions are regarded as hateful." He agreed that he'd seen discrimination so then I asked him, "If there is a real campaign against Christianity to undo the established traditions it has preserved, isn't it possible that this author sees the 'anti-Christian' climate and is either influenced by it or more likely seeking to capitalize off it?" Pete conceded that this was a possibility. I said, "How about if I offered you several books that said the opposite—that the founders were not only Christian but actually, on numerous occasions, consecrated this nation to Almighty God? Which story will you believe?" The question I ask is if we have held these beliefs for our entire history and, similarly, Christians have held them for two millennia, why are we so determined to change them, certain that they are wrong? The answer may be that Christianity stands in the way of people interested in power.

* * *

Don't Be a Slave

"Then Jesus said . . . 'If you continue in my word, you shall be my disciples indeed. And you shall know the truth, and the truth shall make you free.' They answered him: 'We are the seed of Abraham, and we have never been slaves to any man: how sayest thou: you shall be free?' Jesus answered them: 'Amen, amen I say unto you: that whosoever committeth sin, is the servant of sin.'" (John 8:31–34)

It is easy to associate these words with the physical realities of addiction. Today we see more and more things being given the title of 'addiction,' such as video games or the Internet. It is the hard truth to anyone suffering from addiction that they are a slave to that object of addiction, but how many of us are willing to call our bad habits addictions? In this way, every person is a slave to those things that we know are vices and yet do not have the strength to stop. Saint Paul said:

"For many walk . . . enemies of the cross of Christ; whose end is destruction; whose God is their belly; and whose glory is in their shame . . . " (Philippians 3:18–19)

Today, do we worship our stomachs? Maybe we are slaves to our stomachs. And that may be why, first, we are not inclined to change, and second, would abandon Christian truth. The Church points out our sin, making us acknowledge our wrongdoing. Who wants that?!

Many of the founders, on the other hand, were descendants of Christians who escaped Europe to show the world how a land that obeyed the Judeo-Christian law should live and thus be a "city on a hill" to the rest of the world. This was demonstrated not merely because it was a good way to live, but because "God shed his grace"[8] on America.

Our patriots possessed rare attributes and uncommon zeal. *Merriam-Webster Dictionary* defines *revolution* as "the overthrow or renunciation of one government or ruler and the substitution of another by the governed."[9] But the righteousness of a revolution is not measured by the uprising itself because not all, in fact, few, revolutions are good. And any effort to study the American Revolution should also search for the motivations of the Founding Fathers and all the American colonists who fought for this nation whose names are not remembered. Our story is an overall story of freedom, not power.

The accomplishment of these men who overthrew the British Empire is nothing short of miraculous. And we begin to know them just by reading the Declaration of Independence. It is the first document that should be referred to rather than the Constitution, because it reveals the American mind. Then the purpose of the U.S. Constitution becomes clear—the defense of freedom by limiting the power of government.

"When in the course of human events it becomes necessary for one people to dissolve the political bands which have connected them with another, and to assume among the powers of the earth, the separate and equal station to which the Laws of Nature and of Nature's God entitle them, a decent respect to the opinions of mankind requires that they should declare the causes which impel them to the separation."[10]

That separation also helps to understand our revolution. We were not overthrowing the British monarchy, we were separating from them for reasons we felt compelled to share with a candid world so that we would not be judged as anarchists.

This opening paragraph of the Declaration of Independence is intended to be a national collective acknowledgment of Almighty God who has written the laws of nature and thus is the ruler of all nations. It also teaches us that mankind is rightly concerned with revolution; thus, the founders had to distinguish themselves from anarchists so that the world would view them appropriately.

However, the most important thing to be learned by the Declaration of Independence is that our human rights are given to us, not by a benevolent government but by God himself. Governments are only instituted to secure these rights; they are not the origin of them. While everything that they said was true, it neither guaranteed them victory over England nor ensured the future of the new American government.

No extraordinary achievement occurs absent answering an extraordinary challenge, but first it is important to realize both the challenge and the achievement belong to God. Secular society today paints the image of a Utopia and then seeks to eliminate what is not ideal. For example, Denmark has all but eliminated Down syndrome through selective abortions.[11] Human lives are snuffed out for the convenience of those living. This is not an achievement.

The continent of North America was consecrated to our Lord Jesus Christ by Christopher Columbus. Later, the Puritans did likewise when they landed here looking for religious liberty. This country thus begins with Jesus Christ, for it is to Him that the victory that cemented our sovereignty, our freedom, and our prosperity was dedicated. It is clear that the American mind and the American government from its earliest moments believed that Christianity must be integrated into both the structure of government and American society. Look at the following quote from Supreme Court Justice Joseph Story who served on the court from 1812 to 1845:

"It is impossible for those who believe in the Truth of Christianity as a divine revelation to doubt that it is the especial duty of government to foster and encourage it among all the citizens and subjects. This is a point wholly distinct from that of the right of private judgment in matters of religion, and of the freedom of public worship according to the dictates of one's conscience."[12]

This is not a statement to affirm government's role to affirm the truth of a religion, but rather to affirm the truth of the dignity of all people as affirmed by Christianity. Any government that fosters the Truth of Christianity believes, as the founders, in protecting "the dictates of one's conscience."

"Whatever state among us shall continue to make piety and virtue the standard of public honor will enjoy the greatest inward peace, the greatest national happiness, and in every conflict will discover the greatest constitutional strength."[13]
**— John Witherspoon,
signer of the Declaration of Independence**

PART V
COMING HOME

17

AFLOAT WITH NO RUDDER

I N CONTRASTING AMERICA'S BEGINNINGS WITH THE PRESENT DAY, Alexis De Tocqueville provided an unbiased look at our beginning as he traveled America in the 1830s. Once again, as with De Tocqueville, it is good to pay attention to the observations of an unbiased outsider regarding our present state. While reading my son's twelfth-grade history book, I came across the perfect choice—Aleksandr Solzhenitsyn, author of *The Gulag Archipelago,* and outspoken critic of Communism.

At Harvard in 1978, Solzhenitsyn spoke about the plight of modern Western society, about which he made many disturbing observations. This observation by Solzhenitsyn was particularly poignant:

"A decline in courage . . . may be the most striking feature which an outside observer notices in the West in our days . . . Of course there are many courageous individuals but they have no determining influence on public life. Political and intellectual bureaucrats show depression, passivity, and perplexity in their actions and in their statements and even more so in theoretical reflections to explain how realistic, reasonable as well as intellectually and even morally warranted it is to base state policies on weakness and cowardice . . . they get tongue-tied and paralyzed when they deal with powerful governments and threatening forces . . ."[1]

What fosters courageous leadership? Recognizing that early America's sacrifice for liberty was driven by her Christian roots is the most important critical observation. At the heart of Christian teaching is the God-man, Jesus Christ. We learn that He, as God, bore all the physical hardships we experience in this human existence, endured physical torture, and was executed even though He didn't have to allow it. He knowingly endured all of it as God for the purpose of saving every single human being. He does not distinguish one life from another; they are all equal. This supreme act of bravery is the ultimate model for mankind, and it is intended for all because we are all valued the same.

Then, when we read "All men are created equal" in the Declaration of Independence, again we see the value of each individual life as determined by God alone. Christianity, thus, is unique to American government and essential to defending life because it makes equality spiritual, not physical. Abraham Lincoln described succinctly what our sacred purpose is when he said:

" . . . Our fathers brought forth upon this continent, a new nation, conceived in liberty, and dedicated to the proposition that all men are created equal."[2]

A century of attacks on our Christian heritage is destroying the moral compass that has been America's "guiding light" and is eroding the bonds that originally unified us and defined virtue. Prior to that, it was understood that Christianity protected our public morality.

"Christianity is part of the common law of the state, in the qualified sense that it is entitled to respect and protection as the acknowledged religion of the people . . . The claim that the constitutional guarantees of religious liberty are inconsistent with the recognition of Christianity as the religion of the people, is repelled by the known character and history of the framers of the Constitution . . . liberty of conscience is entirely consistent with the existence in fact of the Christian religion, entitled to and enjoying the protection of the law. The public peace and safety are greatly dependent upon the protection of the religion of the country, and the preventing and punishing of offences against it and acts subversive of it."[3] (Justice Allen, decision of the Supreme Court of New York, *Lindenmuller v. The People,* May 29, 1861)

Laws that prohibit prayer in public school or forbid the Ten Commandments in a government building are the symptoms of a culture that is disappearing. If we really served God and acknowledged all He has given us, we would not tolerate any suggestion to remove Him from public life. Without the rudder of our Judeo-Christian roots, American Exceptionalism is being replaced by American indecency, and as a result we can no longer be that "city on a hill" until we rediscover what made us great. Our independence came from *dependence* on God. With like-minded purpose, we gained our freedom, ended slavery, defeated the Nazis, and acted as the true alternative to Communism.

Without God defining morality and freedom, how can Americans be sure of what distinguishes us from the world? This is what separates modern America from its founding. Real courage of our convictions comes from knowing that you are right and those convictions prove their worth, not by being right just for you, but universally right for all of mankind. Aleksandr Solzhenitsyn identified an aspect of American democracy that separated it from the conception of freedom in Western civilization. And that aspect was God. Solzhenitsyn explained modern Western civilization after the Enlightenment saying:

> "This new way of thinking, which had imposed on us its guidance, did not admit the existence of intrinsic evil in man nor did it see any higher task than the attainment of happiness on earth. It based modern Western civilization on the dangerous trend to worship man and his material needs. Everything beyond physical well-being and accumulation of material goods, all other human requirements and characteristics of a subtler and higher nature, were left outside the area of attention of state and social systems, as if human life did not have any superior sense. That provided access for evil, of which in our days there is a free and constant flow."[4]

We are created, as it says in Genesis, by God, in his image and likeness,[5] and as He is obviously free, so are we. Free will and the freedom to choose are never accompanied by coercion.

Abraham Lincoln also wanted to impart on present and future generations a grave challenge, underlined by our Civil War, that any nation conceived on the concept of liberty will be tested, and the response to that test will dictate whether it can endure.

"It is rather for us, the living, we here be dedicated to the great task remaining before us—that from these honored dead we take increased devotion to that cause for which they here, gave the last full measure of devotion that we here highly resolve that these dead shall not have died in vain; that the nation shall have a new birth of freedom, and that government of the people, by the people, for the people, shall not perish from the earth."[6]

The reality recognized by Lincoln, and which should be recognized by us and by future generations, is that the concepts of freedom, equality, and self-government will forever be challenged. That recognition depends on admitting and recognizing good and evil because, hiding in the midst of free society, is evil. Man perverts freedom with lies, changing it to license, and distorts equality, connecting it instead to economic outcomes. The resulting dissension threatens the truth about mankind so that the value of life that underscores America's original purpose is replaced with the value of security, the value of our desires, and a confused conception of rights untethered from any definitive purpose of life.

Americans, unimpeded in a free society that respected the natural law, produced unmatched prosperity for three quarters of our existence, proof that self-government produces prosperity better than any other. Additionally, good and evil individuals have coexisted within our free culture, which gives living proof that, as my father used to say, "The cream rises to the top." In America, good people can gather their efforts for some purpose without the state first identifying that purpose. Yet, this only happens to the extent that we allow it to happen, to the extent that we are able to acknowledge and reward excellence. "Equality of outcomes" empowers authority and works to "homogenize" our society by moving it to the lowest common denominator, thereby creating mediocrity.

Humanity thrives in freedom, but something else is equally true. The moment that we are no longer a Christian nation is the moment that the greatness of America unravels. Why? It is because greatness is achieved through sacrifice, and lofty goals are understood in the context of eternity. Today in America, the loss of Christian teaching is closely followed by the disregard for the natural law. Future generations, individuals not yet born, determine what our country will look like, and the confusion surrounding mother, father, and child is going to create instability in society, an instability that we do not yet see fully. As Solzhenitsyn notes, our freedom depends on our fulfilling our duties to our Creator:

"However, in early democracies, as in American democracy at the time of its birth, all individual human rights were granted because man is God's creature. That is, freedom was given to the individual conditionally, in the assumption of his constant religious responsibility. . . . Even fifty years ago, it would have seemed quite impossible in America that an individual could be granted boundless freedom simply for the satisfaction of his instincts or whims. Subsequently, however, all such limitations were discarded everywhere in the West; a total liberation from the moral heritage of Christian centuries . . ."[7]

Relativism is nothing more than this changing of the hierarchy whereby Man, with all his flaws, moves up to the top of the list, replacing his Creator. The resulting self-centered society succumbs to temptation, replacing responsibility and sacrifice with comfort and pleasure. Solzhenitsyn continues:

"There is a disaster . . . which has already been underway for quite some time. I am referring to the calamity of a despiritualized and irreligious humanistic consciousness. To such consciousness, man is the touchstone in judging and evaluating everything on earth . . . we have lost the concept of a Supreme Complete Entity which used to restrain our passions and our irresponsibility."[8]

Responsibility and sacrifice are necessary ingredients for achievement and courage, and thus a healthy nation is identified by charity and self-sacrifice. This duty to neighbor improves the lives of a nation's citizenry, allowing more people to contribute to society. If America can reunite around our spirituality and our faith in Jesus Christ, we will be at peace—even during hard times. Solzhenitsyn finishes by drawing a similar conclusion:

"If humanism were right in declaring that man was born to be happy, he would not be born to die. Since his body is doomed to die, his task on earth evidently must be of a more spiritual nature. It cannot be unrestrained enjoyment of everyday life . . . It has to be the fulfillment of a permanent, earnest duty so that one's life journey may become an experience of moral growth, so that one may leave life a better human being than one started it . . . Only voluntary, inspired self-restraint can raise man above the world stream of materialism."[9]

There was not a day as a firefighter that I worried about whether my fellow firefighters would be right behind me. We were united as a team to protect life and property. The shared cause of the NYC Fire Department unites firefighters' efforts just the same way as the shared cause of freedom unites America. The key then is to share the same definition of freedom.

To know who we are as a people is to remember our ancestors and where it all began. The first governing document of the American people, the Mayflower Compact, was written by settlers who sought to create a society with freedom to live the Christian life according to their conscience.

"Having undertaken, for the glory of God, and the advancement of the Christian faith . . . a voyage to plant the first colony in the northern parts of Virginia, do by these presents solemnly and mutually in the presence of God, and one another, covenant and combine ourselves together into a civil body politic, for our better ordering and preservation and furtherance of the ends aforesaid . . ."[10]

It is the Gospel's purpose to provide all humanity the truth, thus being a light to all peoples (the governed). And their essential liberty is an intended component of their created being. This principle was, for the first time in the history of the world, protected by a governing proclamation when the Declaration of Independence was presented to the world. Thus, the United States forever has the task of protecting the concepts of individual freedom—a task that has caused us to be hated by many tyrannical governments over the course of our history, yet respected by its people. Today, however, we find that it is the peoples of the world who are demonstrating hatred for America as we slowly begin to resemble those tyrannical regimes, abandoning the very reason for our American Revolution— the forming of a government "of, by, and for the people"—a people created with equal value regardless of their gifts.

> **"It is a well-known fact that no virtuous people were ever oppressed, and it is also true that a scourge was never wanting to those of an opposite character."**[11] (John Jay)

*　*　*

Heroes Are a Mighty Obstacle to Exploitation!
Great leaders, who inspire people to overcome great obstacles or achieve great things, are but one kind of hero. More important, because they are in our midst, are the everyday heroes. They inspire individuals by virtue of their example, whether it's their work ethic, their charity, etc., to raise the bar and be better than they could ever imagine. It is for this reason that they have been the target of evil intentions, to usurp people for power and wealth, because heroes are a mighty obstacle to exploitation.

Current overreaching policies are whittling away at the return of these great individuals' efforts. Everyone knows from personal experience that some projects are extremely tiring and frustrating, yet we persevere because of the satisfaction we receive in the finished result. It seems logical to me that if one removes the finished result, they have also removed the motivation for the endeavor. On the broad scale, entitlement policies employed by a large government bureaucracy do just that. They create a welfare state—a society where individuals no longer feel empowered and self-sufficient and thus surrender "pieces" of their liberty. This aim sees only physical sustenance and not the spiritual sustenance that is part of our American heritage, a spiritual sustenance that makes irrelevant the benevolence of the government.

A proliferation of American heroes, rivaling the product of a whole millennium, is the by-product of the "American Way," and it is American heroes who can pull us out of our current decline. However, this can only happen if they are defined by their moral courage rather than a personal exalting and, most especially, can only happen if they are visible. Unless we once again correctly recognize as 'hero,' not the individual who proclaims his/her own greatness but the man/woman who has sacrificed their own luxury, safety, or even life for a goal greater than themselves, we will never relive the prosperity of the past. This greater goal of true freedom from which all people benefit will use our potential to improve as we have throughout our history. It is, in fact, that American potential to improve our lot in life through diligence that brought appreciative immigrants pouring onto our shores. They recognized that the American Way embraced the individual's right to the "pursuit of happiness," not the Socialist promise of happiness guaranteed by the welfare state. They knew that bigotry and hatred, inherent in the human condition, did not miraculously disappear here, but that now those human evils were addressed in a unique form of government built to protect against them. If we recognize what truly makes a hero and we see Christ as our model, we will choose the hard road with its reward, and our best days are yet to come.

Socialism preys on our innate human weakness, especially the tendency to take the easiest road without examining the long-term consequences. Solzhenitsyn, whose life was harsh and who lived outside of the West, made this observation about guaranteed well-being:

"Even biology knows that habitual extreme safety and well-being are not advantageous for a living organism."[12]

As America continues in this direction, she will feel a loss of confidence, hope, and dreams that have been the hallmark of our country, trading the 'can do' attitude for security and transforming progress into dependency on the state. The motivations of ease and security, in place of a biblical work ethic and self-sacrifice, are contrary to both the American founding and American Exceptionalism, and they must be resisted. Solzhenitsyn continues his observations on, what I agree, is a culture in peril:

> "And yet . . . no weapons, no matter how powerful, can help the West until it overcomes its loss of willpower. In a state of psychological weakness, weapons become a burden for the capitulating side. To defend oneself, one must also be ready to die; there is little such readiness in a society raised in the cult of material well-being."[13]

* * *

Restoring Virtue

Elected officials are only a reflection of the people they represent. Any weakness in them is a byproduct of the voting public from which they come. Obviously, there will never be a perfect candidate, and so we are left with a weighty decision and must set our priorities. Still, if people are not led by a set of timeless principles, their vote becomes vulnerable to immediate whims, with no regard to long-term consequences. Without defined principles, our criteria can change in hard times with the danger being the natural temptation to take the easiest road and select representatives who promise us relief from our distress. Judeo-Christian tradition is focused on man's eternal well-being. So, its goals are meant for the long haul. Its guidance is meant to steer us away from short-term temptations. And without Judeo-Christian tradition that assigns us a duty to our neighbor, we are left to our own reason, which is inclined to see our own good. And it was the belief of our founders not to select the easiest road, but the more principled one that reflects the greater good. George Washington says the price of virtue is more than repaid.

"Observe good faith and justice toward all nations; cultivate peace and harmony with all. Religion and morality enjoin this conduct; and can it be, that good policy does not equally enjoin it? . . . It will be worthy of a free, enlightened, and at no distant, a great nation to give to mankind the magnanimous and too novel example of the people always guided by an exalted justice and benevolence. Who can doubt that, in the course of time and things, the fruits of such a plan would richly repay any temporary advantages, which might be lost by a steady adherence to it? Can it be that Providence has not connected the permanent felicity of the nation with its virtue? The experiment, at least, is recommended by every sentiment which ennobles human nature. Alas! Is it rendered impossible by its vices?"[14]

The problem is that the choices for public office usually fall short of this moral yardstick and we must compromise to get the best servant from those running for office. But we do have a hierarchy of principles given to us by the founders that cannot be compromised. They are first, life; second, liberty; and third, the pursuit of happiness—in that order.

Since our politicians come from amongst us, we will not see these values in them unless they are first in us. As mentioned earlier, the root of sin is human pride. For these Christian values to be seen in our society, we will need to embrace humility because it is the opposite of pride. People cannot be perfect, but we can, as Washington suggests, be "guided by an exalted justice and benevolence" starting with a humble appreciation of God.

"We should always remember that the many and unexpected means and events by which our wants have been supplied and our enemies repelled or restrained are such strong and striking proofs of the interposition of Heaven, that our having been hitherto delivered from the threatened bondage of Britain ought to be forever ascribed to its true cause (the favor of God), and, instead of swelling our breasts with arrogant ideas of our prowess and importance, kindle in them a flame of gratitude and piety which may consume all remains of vice and irreligion."[15] (John Jay)

A culture cannot survive the test of time without its members depending on each other. This requires a degree of trust in their good and common intention, yet this is not to be construed with dependency. Depending on and trusting each other is the way human beings operating in solidarity solve the problems of the day. This unity breeds strength. To depend on means to count on and implies integrity and sacrifice, setting aside personal goals, comforts, or prosperity for a greater good.

This is why the success of culture depends on Christianity, not only because of its moral teachings, which are true, but because of the example of the Cross of the Son of God.

Pope John Paul II emphasized that God's love for you is proven in the Cross because Jesus did not have to come, suffer as a man, and die, but did so out of love for his creation. Without this example, the idea of God's love would be unfounded and our own suffering meaningless. With this example, we are inspired to sacrifice for each other. This command of Jesus is already proven to produce good fruit. When we compare our finite human life with eternity, we take the important first step in prioritizing. Our current time of national crisis is absolutely linked to the moral crisis that comes from disconnecting our society from our maker, where desire has replaced responsibility. To recognize heroes forces us to evaluate ourselves. In contrast, ignoring them condemns us to mediocrity at best. Robert Kennedy reflected on his brother Jack's fondness for quoting Dante, saying:

"The hottest places in hell are reserved for those who, in a time of great moral crisis, maintain their neutrality."[16]

It is, in fact, in striving for excellence, contrary to what we hear today, that we live out our freedoms. Naturally, this requires effort on our part, the motivation to achieve. Yet, why should anyone want to achieve? Why not just flounder in mediocrity living a life of ease? The belief that God created life should force us to reflect on the purpose for our own life, ultimately leading us back to what his purpose for our life was. We do not exist merely to continue to exist. So then, what is our own life all about except to use our talents and strength in service to society? That is what makes life satisfying. It really makes us relevant.

The quest for personal excellence can be contrasted with

the acceptance of personal mediocrity, or worse, the loathing of excellence in others because of envy. Once we lose sight of the knowledge of our Creator who fashioned us as we are and loves us as we are, the beauty of others is diminished and their talent becomes only a reminder of what we are lacking.

"The energies and talents of all of us are needed to meet the challenges . . . Pleasantries, self-satisfied mediocrity will serve us badly. We need the best of many, not just a few. We must strive for excellence."[17] (Robert Kennedy)

The concept of personal excellence depends on the fact that we are a created being. It is underscored every time we acknowledge that someone is gifted, because it also assumes that the individual did not choose the 'gift.' While both are geniuses, Beethoven and Einstein are not interchangeable. Their excellence is dependent on their exploring their unique gifts. Our interdependence as human beings is illustrated by this realization. If Beethoven, for instance, had written the Fifth Symphony and then hid it in a shoe box in his closet, although he would be free to do it, it is naturally wrong. The symphony's excellence, the source of his personal satisfaction, could not be known because without others hearing it, there would be nothing against which to measure it. The same holds true for Einstein or any other genius, and even for others whose talents might not be that exceptional.

For a society, this concept of "freedom of excellence" is even more critical. Poor individual choices are singular losses, but when outside forces coerce the population, as in Communism, the losses are widespread. If Beethoven could be ordered to become a baker, or Einstein a coal miner, then the society at large has lost its ability to pursue excellence. The results capable by the freeman can never be achieved under

Communism/Socialism because the drive for excellence is in conflict with lust for power. American Exceptionalism is dependent on American liberty.

∗ ∗ ∗

The Fountain of Youth

Everyone remembers the story of Ponce de Leon seeking the Fountain of Youth. Throughout history, mankind has been obsessed with finding a fountain of youth to end the fear of our own mortality. The appeal of this elixir, of course, is not to the young, who feel invincible, but rather to we who, like Ponce de Leon, do not want their vitality to slip away. The longer we live, the more missed opportunities we see, along with the bitter realization that we are running out of the time and energy to realize our dreams. If only youth were not wasted on the young!

But for nations, the fountain of youth is not a myth. Newness and excitement are an everyday reality when people live in freedom. When we think of youth, we think of growth and energy, fearlessness, and hope. America guaranteed herself this perpetual energy by embracing individual liberty. Free thought never runs short of creative dreams and new ideas, and the excitement grows as the dreams are realized. Serving God in the creation of a free nation had the secondary benefits of the continuous newness of human ideas. This end is implied in God's command noted in the book of Genesis, "Be fruitful and multiply, and fill the earth and subdue it." (Genesis 1:28)

18

THE PRODIGAL NATION

"It is the duty of all Nations to acknowledge the Providence of Almighty God, to obey his will, to be grateful for his benefits, and humbly to implore his protection and favor." [1]
— **President George Washington**

I HAVE MADE A PRAGMATIC CASE THAT AMERICA WAS FIRST A DEMONSTRATION of a system of government that recognized its reliance on God, while examining the relationship between that reliance and her climb to exceptionalism, an exceptionalism that is waning today. What has been the effect of extracting the Christian environment in favor of secularism in the public sphere? More important, is there a supernatural consequence to this? If the rise of America is linked to God's approval, what can result from detaching ourselves from Him?

The fact that my supernatural conclusion will not influence anyone attached to the modern secular progressive movement is a critical point. Our ancestors recognized both divine Providence and divine judgment. The question is: "What can we do without God?"

"Every one that heareth these my words, and doth them not, shall be like a foolish man who built his house upon the sand. And the rains fell, and the floods came, and the winds blew, and they beat upon that house, and it fell, and great was the fall thereof." (Matthew 7:26-27)

With the mounting problems this country is facing, it is critical that we look once again to God, not just with the goal of restoring our economic prosperity but also to preserve individual liberty! The truth about American Exceptionalism begins with the truth about mankind. Thus, to recognize, understand, and defend truths concerning—for instance—marriage, human sexuality, the sanctity of life, or simply our responsibilities to each other, we must first recognize and surrender to the One who created us in the first place.

Much of this treatise has pointed out how our departure from our Judeo-Christian heritage has led us to errors in judgment. But the most important thing we need to take from this discussion is to acknowledge the hand of Almighty God. Regardless of the things we choose to debate, the wisdom for the debate comes from the same place. We have one sure hope guaranteed to correct the current self-destructive course. The solution is to simply turn around and come home, to look for the things that God demands of us and incorporate them into our solutions. The Founding Fathers testified to His aid, as seen in the Great Seal of the United States, and numerous public statements, and there is reasonable expectation that, if America can turn sorrowfully and move to the Creator, the Creator will respond favorably with his mercy.

The definition of *repentance* is "voluntary sorrow because it (sin) offends God . . . together with resolve to amend one's conduct."[2] If you are on the wrong course, you make no progress until you turn around. Jesus gives us the Parable of the

Prodigal Son to show what we can expect when we sincerely change, turn around, and come home to where we belong.

"A man had two sons, and the younger son said to his father, 'Father, give me the share of your estate that should come to me.' So the father divided the property between them. After a few days, the younger son collected all his belongings and set off to a distant country where he squandered his inheritance on a life of dissipation." (Luke 15:11-13)

An analogy can here be made with America replacing the prodigal son. America lives by its Judeo-Christian heritage and partakes then of the prosperity that comes only from God, just as the son lives in accord with the father and thereby has a right to inheritance from Him. And America, like the son, leaves the home of her birth, squandering her inheritance, exceptionalism. The parable continues:

"When he had freely spent everything, a severe famine struck that country, and he found himself in dire need. So he hired himself out to one of the local citizens, who sent him to his farm to tend the swine." (Luke 15:14-15)

Through the character of the son, Jesus illustrates, first, the result of his decadence, absolute poverty. His lifestyle, however, robs him of more than just his inheritance. He has also lost his freedom. This is the critical connection to our present situation. There is nothing Americans identify with more than freedom. The moral poverty of the son led to his physical poverty which, in turn, forced him to subject himself to the controls of another. Likewise, America, in moving toward secularism and away from Christian governing principles, is moving toward despotism and away from freedom. There is a moral connection, as we squander our assets, to the prodigal son who foolishly spends everything with no conception of the future, finally leaving himself at the mercy of a neighbor to feed him scraps worthy of a pig. He never foresaw his future starvation because he had never learned from his father.

"And he longed to eat his fill of the pods on which the swine fed, but nobody gave him any." (Luke 15:16)

The Cato Institute has been compiling data to rate both human freedom and economic freedom. The report from 2015 reveals some very disturbing facts. The Human Freedom Index (HFI) found:

"The top 10 jurisdictions in order were Hong Kong, Switzerland, Finland, Denmark, New Zealand, Canada, Australia, Ireland, the United Kingdom, and Sweden. The United States is ranked in 20th place."[3]

We then ranked in 23rd place in 2016 and 17th place in 2017 and 2018.

Economic freedom didn't do much better. The 2015 report stated:

"The United States, once considered a bastion of economic freedom, now ranks sixteenth in the world with a score of 7.73. Due to a weakening rule of law, increasing regulation, and the ramifications of wars on terrorism and drugs, the United States has seen its economic freedom score plummet in recent years, compared to 2000 when it ranked second globally."[4]

It was revised in the 2016 report:

"Global economic freedom increased slightly in this year's report to 6.85. Hong Kong and Singapore retain the top two positions with a score of 9.03 and 8.71 out of 10, respectively. The rest of this year's top scores are New Zealand, 8.35; Switzerland, 8.25; Canada, Georgia, Ireland, Mauritius, and the United Arab Emirates at 7.98; and Australia and the United Kingdom at 7.93.

The United States, once considered a bastion of economic

freedom, ranks sixteenth for a second consecutive year with a score of 7.75."[5]

The most recent years, however, show improvement. The 2017 report says, "The United States, for decades among the top four countries in the index, ranks 11th." And the 2018 report puts us in 6th place. It is good to ask what is responsible for the positive movement because people's lives are seriously affected by their economic freedom. The same report also compiled the following facts:

"Nations in the top quartile of economic freedom had an average per capita GDP of US $42,463 in 2015, compared to $6,036 for bottom quartile nations. Moreover, the average income of the poorest 10 percent in the most economically free nations is almost twice the average per capita income in the least free nations. Life expectancy is 80.7 years in the top quartile compared to 64.4 years in the bottom quartile and political and civil liberties are considerably higher in economically free nations than in unfree nations."[6]

In the media, the bulk of the economic warnings center around our devastating national debt, but debt is just one of the many symptoms of a spreading moral poverty. The Cato Institute identifies, in the quote above, "a weakening rule of law" and "increasing regulation" as contributors to our diminishing economic freedom. Yet it seems folly to answer the frustration of a weakening rule of law by enacting more law in the way of regulation. The inevitable fatal result of this growing regulation is the arbitrary exercise of its force, with very little difference in effect than the tyranny of the despot. Further, the disappearance of temperance suggested by our increased debt is also reflected in the war on drugs— a war only necessary because of an unchecked appetite for vice. Just as a disease runs rampant in the weakened host, so does terrorism spread through a morally impoverished society.

The prodigal son, on his path to ruin, met many individuals very willing to entertain his lusts, none of whom were concerned for his well-being. Rather, they gladly encouraged him to spend every last penny on his depravity. Is it any different for America? In the same way, this country will be continuously encouraged to spend every penny of her 'inheritance' until we are ruined; therefore, the impetus for our national recovery must come from within us from the depths of our spirit.

"Coming to his senses, he thought, 'How many of my father's workers have more than enough food to eat, but here am I, dying of hunger.' I shall get up and go to my father and I shall say to him, 'Father, I have sinned against heaven and against you. I no longer deserve to be called your son; treat me as you would treat one of your hired workers.' So he got up and went back to his father. While he was still a way off, his father caught sight of him, and was filled with compassion. He ran to his son, embraced him, and kissed him." (Luke 15:7-20)

With the advance of a Godless culture, the public debate is increasingly relegated to economics, but the founders of our nation were not motivated by economic prosperity. On the contrary, their zeal was for individual liberty. They believed to be protected from the rule of the tyrant they must coalesce to the rule of the Creator, the source of all truth and all law. Once this country acknowledges its departure from His law, America will have taken the first step in identifying the cause of her decline and the path back to exceptionalism. What follows in the story of the prodigal son is intended by Jesus Christ to be a revelation that both teaches America what it must do to regain her exceptionalism and what we can look forward to as a result.

"His son said to him, 'Father, I have sinned against heaven and against you; I no longer deserve to be called your son.' But his father ordered his servants, 'Quickly bring the finest robe and put it on him; put a ring on his finger and sandals on his feet. Take the fatted calf and slaughter it. Then let us celebrate with a feast, because this son of mine was dead, and has come to life again; he was lost and has been found.' Then the celebration began . . . " (Luke 15:21-23)

There is assuredly a feast that awaits us, and any nation for that matter, that can turn around and return in humility to God. It is not an American recipe for success but a universal one. This turnaround is the recognition of His authority over us and our submission to that authority. A speech given by Benjamin Franklin at the Constitutional Convention on June 28, 1787, which was met with unanimous approval, is applicable to our current struggles. Up until that point, those at the Convention were divided and discouraged, but the outcome is well known. It is the modern United States that is a victim of her own pride, but our ancestors depended on Providence for the success of the United States. Franklin said:

"We have gone back to ancient history for models of government, and examined the different forms of those republics which, having been formed with the seeds of their own destruction, now no longer exist . . . "

"In this situation of this assembly, groping as it were in the dark to find political truth and scarce able to distinguish it when presented to us, how has it happened, sir, that we have not hitherto once thought of humbly applying to the Father of lights to illuminate our understanding? In the beginning of the contest with Great Britain, when we were sensible of danger, we had daily prayers in this room for the Divine protection. Our prayers, sir, were heard, and they were graciously answered. All of us who were engaged in the struggle must have observed frequent instances of a superintending Providence in our favor. To that kind Providence we owe this happy opportunity of consulting in peace on the means of establishing our future national felicity. And have we now forgotten that powerful Friend? Or do we imagine that we no longer need his assistance?

"I have lived, sir, a long time, and the longer I live, the more convincing proofs I see of this truth—that God governs in the affairs of men. And if a sparrow cannot fall to the ground without his notice, is it probable that an empire can rise without his aid? We have been assured, sir, in the sacred writings, that 'Except the Lord build the house they labor in vain that build it.' I firmly believe this; and I also believe that without His concurring aid we shall succeed in this political building no better than the builders of Babel. We shall be divided by our little, partial, local interests; our projects will be confounded, and we ourselves become a reproach and byword down to future ages. And what is worse, mankind may hereafter, from this unfortunate circumstance, despair of establishing governments by human wisdom, and leave it to chance, war, and conquest.

"I therefore beg leave to move that henceforth prayers imploring the assistance of Heaven, and its blessings on our deliberations, be held in this assembly every morning before we proceed to business, and that one or more of the clergy of this city be requested to officiate in that service."[7]

After our Constitution was finally adopted, Benjamin Morris recounts a procession in Philadelphia to honor the new Constitution:

"At Philadelphia, twenty thousand people met and welcomed Washington with cries of, 'Long live George Washington! Long live the father of our country!' Washington ... spoke as follows, 'When I contemplate the interposition of Providence, as it has been visibly manifested in guiding us through the Revolution, in preparing us for the General Government, and in conciliating the good will of the people of America toward one another in its adoption, I feel myself oppressed and overwhelmed with a sense of Divine munificence.' "[8]

Today, the great task ahead of us begins with an about-face that will require a very difficult departure from our own pride and complacency and a concerted march back to the Judeo-Christian tradition that has accompanied every exceptional work of America. American Exceptionalism is from a recipe available universally to every nation—Nature's Law. May God accept this essay as a prayer to the Holy Spirit that asks for forgiveness and a new enlightenment.

"This is what is called the law of nature, which, ... being coeval with mankind and dictated by God Himself, is, of course, superior in obligation to any other. No human laws are of any validity if contrary to this. It is binding over all the globe, in all countries, and at all times." (Alexander Hamilton)[9]

NOTES

Introduction

1. *Kolbe 12th Grade History, Modern History Reader* (Napa, California: Kolbe Academy, 2008), 381.

2. Harris, Alex, and Brett Harris, *Do Hard Things*, foreword by Chuck Norris (Colorado Springs, Colorado: Multnomah Books, 2013), xiii.

3. Morris, Benjamin F., *The Christian Life and Character of the Civil Institutions of the United States* (Powder Springs, Georgia: American Vision, Inc., 2007), 185.

Chapter 1: What Is Exceptional?

1. Sheen, Fulton J., *Whence Come Wars* (New York: Sheen and Ward, 1940), 112.

2. The slogan used by President-elect Donald Trump in his 2016 presidential campaign.

3. De Tocqueville, Alexis, *Democracy in America, Vol. 1*, Chapter XVII: "Principal Causes Which Tend to Maintain the Democratic Republic in the United States," http://xroads.virginia.edu/~Hyper/DETOC/religion/ch1_17.htm, accessed April 18, 2017.

4. *Kolbe 12th Grade History, Modern History Reader*, 381.

5. The *American Heritage College Dictionary* defines deism as "the belief, based on reason, in a God who created the universe and has since assumed no control over life, exerted no influence on nature, and given no supernatural revelation."

6. Morris, Benjamin F., *The Christian Life and Character*, 251–254.

7. Ibid., 245. Daniel Webster (1782–1852) served as Representative, Senator, and Secretary of State and was considered one of the greatest orators up until that point in American history.

8. "Amendment I: Congress shall make no law respecting an establishment of religion, or prohibiting the free exercise thereof . . . "

9. Morris, 257. The author cites from Rev. Dr. Strickland's *History of the American Bible Society*.

10. *Time* Magazine, National Affairs: "Eisenhower on Communism," October 13, 1952, Vol. LX No. 15.

11. Speech at the National Day of Prayer, May 6, 1982.

12. Morris, 143.

13. Sheen, *Whence Come Wars*, 3.

14. From paragraph 2, line 1 of the Declaration of Independence, in Congress, July 4, 1776.

15. "John Locke, The Works of John Locke, Vol. 1 (An Essay Concerning Human Understanding Part 1) [1689]," Chapter XXI, part 56, "Online Library of Liberty, A Collection of Scholarly Works about Individual Liberty and Free Markets," Liberty Fund, Inc., accessed September 29, 2016, http://oll.libertyfund.org/titles/locke-the-works-vol-1-an-essay-concerning-human-understanding-part-1

16.   Hayek, Friedrich A., *The Road to Serfdom: Text and Documents/* F. A. Hayek; ed. Bruce Caldwell—The Definitive Edition (Routledge, London: The University of Chicago Press, 2007), 156.

Chapter 2: The Great Seal

1.   William Federer, American Minute with Bill Federer, accessed December 20, 2018, https://myemail.constantcontact.com/-I-had-four-bullets-through-my-coat---two-horses-shot-under-me--yet-escaped-unhurt---George-Washington.html?soid=1108762609255&aid=OGcBTiF7VcA

2.   MacArthur, John D., Great Seal.com, "First Great Seal Committee—July/August 1776," http://greatseal.com/committees/firstcomm/index.html

3.   MacArthur, Great Seal.com, "Explanation of the Great Seal's Symbolism," http://greatseal.com/committees/firstcomm/index.html

4.   Schecter, Barnet, *The Battle for New York, The City at the Heart of the American Revolution* (New York: Walker & Company, 2002), 165.

5.   Bradshaw, Wesley, "Washington's Dream," The *National Tribune*, December 1, 1880.

6.   MacArthur, Great Seal.com, "The Great Seal of the United States, An Overview by John D. MacArthur," http://greatseal.com/committees/firstcomm/index.html

7.   Morris, Benjamin F., *The Christian Life and Character*, 145.

8.   founders.archives.gov/documents/Washington/03-16-02-0373

9.   National Archives, Founders Online: From George Washington to John Armstrong, 11 March 1792; accessed

July 29, 2018, https://founders.archives.gov/documents/Washington/05-10-02-0044

10. Morris, 168.

Chapter 3: The Supreme Sacrifice

1. From the inscription at the Firemen's Memorial, Riverside Drive and West 100th Street, Manhattan.

2. "Three Forms of Love," Landon Lecture Series on Public Issues, Kansas State University, March 16, 1970, Venerable Fulton J. Sheen, Archbishop of the Titular See of Newport (Wales), https://www.k-state.edu/landon/speakers/fulton-sheen/transcript.html

3. Ibid.

4. The Declaration of Independence.

5. George Washington's Inaugural Address of 1789, https://www.archives.gov/exhibits/american_originals/inaugtxt.html

6. From the preamble to the Constitution of the United States of America.

7. Morris, Benjamin F., *The Christian Life and Character,* 71–72.

8. Ibid., 162.

9. The mask is a self-contained breathing apparatus (SCBA) with a tank filled with purified air.

10. The phrase is anecdotally attributed to Benjamin Franklin just before signing the Declaration of Independence, 1776.

11. See http://www.ufoa.org/, accessed January 23, 2017.

12. November 13, 1787, letter to William S. Smith, quoted in Padover's "Jefferson On Democracy," ed., 1939,

http://books.google.com/books?id=imMmIlv1G7MC&pg=PA268&q=&f=false#v=onepage&q=&f=false

13. Ibid.

14. Sheen, Fulton J., *Whence Come Wars*, 11–12.

15. The Declaration of Independence.

16. Sheen, 102, 104.

Chapter 4: The Crossroads

1. The Declaration of Independence.

2. Sheen, Fulton J., *Whence Come Wars*, 62–63.

3. Website: John F. Kennedy Presidential Library and Museum, "John F. Kennedy Quotations: President Kennedy's Inaugural Address, January 20, 1961," http://www.jfklibrary.org/Research/Research-Aids/Ready-Reference/JFK-Quotations/Inaugural-Address.aspx

4. Federer, William J., *What Every American Needs to Know About the Qur'an: A History of Islam and the United States* (St. Louis: Amerisearch, Inc., 2014), 193, 194, 195, 197. William Federer quotes Theodore Roosevelt from his book, *Fear God and Take Your Own Part* (New York: George H. Doran Co., 1916).

5. Morris, Benjamin F., *The Christian Life and Character*, 144.

6. Kennedy, John F., "The President and the Press" Speech (April 27, 1961). President Kennedy speaks at the Waldorf-Astoria Hotel in New York City before the American Newspaper Publishers Association, https://www.jfklibrary.org/archives/other-resources/john-f-kennedy-speeches/american-newspaper-publishers-association-19610427

7. De Tocqueville, Alexis, *Democracy in America, Vol. 1,*

translated by Henry Reeve, Esq., (New York: George Ad-lard, 1839) 52.

8. Website: John F. Kennedy Presidential Library and Museum: John F. Kennedy Speeches, "The President and the Press: Address before the American Newspaper Publishers Association, April 27, 1961," http://www.jfklibrary.org/Research/Research-Aids/JFK-Speeches/American-Newspaper-Publishers-Association_19610427.aspx

9. Website: ushistory.org, "The Electric Franklin: The Quotable Franklin," http://www.ushistory.org/franklin/quotable/quote04.htm

    In 1755 (Pennsylvania Assembly: Reply to the Governor, Tue, Nov 11, 1755), Franklin wrote: "Those who would give up essential Liberty, to purchase a little temporary Safety, deserve neither Liberty nor Safety."

    This phrasing was also the motto in Historical Review of Pennsylvania, attributed to Franklin. It's important to note that this sentiment, with many variations, was much used in the Revolutionary Period by Franklin and others.

10. John Paul II, Pope, *Crossing the Threshold of Hope*, ed. Vittorio Messori (New York: Alfred A. Knopf, Inc.), 62.

Chapter 5: The Hero's Cross

1. Morris, Benjamin F., *The Christian Life and Character*, 167.

2. Sheen, Fulton J., *Whence Come Wars*, 9.

3. The Declaration of Independence.

4. Ibid.

5. Genesis 1:26-27: "26 And He said: Let us make man to our image and likeness . . . 27 And God created man to His own image: to the image of God He created him:

male and female He created them."

6. https://www.britannica.com/topic/Buddhism Accessed January 12, 2019.

7. Mlb.com, Doug Miller, "Inspired by Daughter, Carew Impacting Lives," http://m.mlb.com/news/article/67298014/inspired-by-daughter-hall-of-famer-rod-carew-impacting-lives

8. Morris, 146.

9. The Declaration of Independence.

Chapter 6: Assault on Heroes

1. Morris, Benjamin F., *The Christian Life and Character*, 156.

2. The Declaration of Independence.

3. Morris, 175.

4. From Abraham Lincoln's speech: "The Perpetuation of Our Political Institutions: Address before the Young Men's Lyceum of Springfield, Illinois," January 27, 1838, www.abrahamlincoln.org/lincoln/speeches/lyceum.htm, accessed January 20, 2019.

5. Lee, Tony, "Reid: 'Radical' 'Tea Party Anarchists' Holding Gov't 'Hostage,' " Breitbart, September 23, 2013, http://www.breitbart.com/Big-Government/2013/09/23/Reid-Radical-Tea-Party-Anarchists-Holding-Gov-t-Hostage

6. *Kolbe Modern History Reader*, 385.

7. Reagan, Ronald, "Encroaching Control," given before the Phoenix Chamber of Commerce on March 30, 1961, https://archive.org/details/RonaldReagan-Encroaching Control Accessed January 20, 2019.

8. Hayek, F. A., *The Road to Serfdom*, 175.

9. President John F. Kennedy speaking at the Waldorf-Astoria Hotel, New York City, April 27, 1961, to the National Newspaper Guild.

10. Hayek, F. A., *The Constitution of Liberty: The Definitive Edition*, ed. by Ronald Hamowy, (Chicago: The University of Chicago Press, 1960), 65.

11. Reagan, "A Time for Choosing," televised campaign address for the Goldwater presidential campaign, October 27, 1964, https://www.reaganlibrary.gov/timechoosing Accessed January 20, 2019.

12. Roosevelt, Theodore, "Man in the Arena" speech, given April 23, 1910.

Chapter 7: The Home of the Brave

1. Outside vent is one of the positions for Ladder Company personnel. They have the very dangerous position of laddering, timed ventilation of the fire floor opposite the charged hose line, and entering to search for victims.

2. Morris, Benjamin F., *The Christian Life and Character*, 223. This is an excerpt of a letter from Andrew Jackson to Commodore Elliott, who brought a sarcophagus from Asia as a gift to him. He humbly stated, "I cannot permit my remains to be the first in these United States to be deposited in a sarcophagus made for an emperor or a king . . . "

3. Meyer, Joyce, *The Confident Woman Devotional: 365 Daily Inspirations*, (New York: FaithWords Hachette Book Group, 2010), 133.

4. Genesis 2:18: "And the Lord God said: it is not good for man to be alone: let us make him a help like unto himself."

5. Stated by John Winthrop in 1632 to the Massachusetts Bay colonists,; he links our founding and exceptionalism to our dedication to Christian ideals. January 9, 1961,

President-Elect John F. Kennedy used the phrase during an address delivered to the General Court of Massachusetts as did President Ronald Reagan in his 1984 acceptance of the Republican Party nomination.

Chapter 8: Our Most Valuable Asset

1. www.hslda.org/hs/international/Sweden/201503240.asp

2. Morris, Benjamin F., *The Christian Life and Character*, 223. Excerpt of a letter from Andrew Jackson to Commodore Elliott.

3. George Washington's Farewell Address, 1796, Yale Law School, Lillian Goldman Law Library, The Avalon Project: Documents in Law, History and Diplomacy 2008, http://avalon.law.yale.edu/18th_century/washing.asp

4. Hayek, F. A., *The Constitution of Liberty: The Definitive Edition*, edited by Ronald Hamowy (Chicago: The University of Chicago Press, 1960), 69 n. 28. Hayek quotes Bronislaw Malinowski, *Freedom and Civilization* (New York: Roy Publishers, 1944), 47.

5. Wallbuilders, "Is America a Christian Nation?" by David Barton, accessed February 22, 2017, https://wallbuilders.com/america-christian-nation/

6. Patrick Henry, May 1765 Speech to the House of Burgesses.

7. The Witherspoon Institute, Natural Law, Natural Rights, and American Constitutionalism, Letter from Birmingham Jail (Martin Luther King, Jr.), accessed October 13, 2016, http://www.nlnrac.org/american/american-civil-rights-movements/primary-source-documents/letter-from-a-birmingham-jail

8. Morris, Benjamin F., *The Christian Life and Character of the Civil Institutions of the United States,* 187.

Chapter 9: Judeo-Christian Heroism

1. Morris, Benjamin F., *The Christian Life and Character of the Civil Institutions of the United States*, 153–154.

2. Ibid., 832.

3. Dwight Eisenhower is quoted in the *Time* Magazine article, National Affairs: "Eisenhower on Communism," October 13, 1952, Vol. LX No. 15.

4. William J. Federer discussed the different meaning of the word *deist* from the time of our founding to today in a recorded interview. See DVD disk 4, "History Speaks: What Makes Democracy Work: Deism, Ben Franklin & Presidents on Faith", (Bloomingdale, OH: Apostolate for Family Consecration, 2006).

5. *Encarta Dictionary: English* (North America).

6. George Washington's Inaugural Address of 1789, https://www.archives.gov/exhibits/american_originals/inaugtxt.html

7. William J. Federer discussed the "Separation of Church and State" in a recorded interview. See DVD disk 2, "History Speaks: What Makes Democracy Work: Historical Analysis of Jefferson's Letter to the Danbury Baptists" (Bloomingdale, OH: Apostolate for Family Consecration, 2006).

8. Morris, *The Christian Life and Character*, 66.

9. Ibid., 65.

10. President Kennedy's Inaugural Address, January 20, 1961, from the John F. Kennedy Presidential Library and Museum, accessed October 3, 2016, http://www.jfklibrary.org/AssetViewer/BqXIEM9F4024ntFl7SVAjA.aspx

Chapter 10: True Law Is Absolute

1. Cicero, Marcus Tullius, "On the Commonwealth," in James E. G. Zetzel, ed., *On the Commonwealth and On the Laws* (Cambridge: Cambridge University Press, 1999), 71–72.

2. Rutler, George W., Father, "A River in Egypt: Denying the Undeniable," *Crisis Magazine*, June 16, 2016, http://www.crisismagazine.com/2016/river-egypt-denying- undeniable#.V2Kd0PdHhbw.mailto

3. Acton Institute, Lord Acton Quote Archive, http://www.acton.org/research/lord-acton-quote-archive

4. Morris, *The Christian Life and Character of the Civil Institutions of the United States*, 179.

5. Abraham Lincoln's Gettysburg Address.

6. Shlichta, Paul, "The Roots of Liberalism and Conservatism," *American Thinker*, December 26, 2011, http://www.americanthinker.com/articles/2011/12/the_r oots_of_liberalism_and_conservatism.html

7. "Founding Father Quotes: Quotes, Biographies, and Writings of the Founding Fathers," http://www.foundingfatherquotes.com/father/id/11

8. Morris, *The Christian Life and Character*, 145.

9. John F. Kennedy Presidential Library and Museum, Inaugural Address of President John F. Kennedy, Washington, D.C., January 20, 1961, paragraph 2, accessed March 29, 2017, https://www.jfklibrary.org/Research/Research-Aids/Ready-Reference/JFK-Quotations/Inaugural-Address.aspx

10. John Locke, http://oll.libertyfund.org/titles/locke-the-works-vol-1-an-essay-concerning-human-understanding-part-1

11. Morris, 142.

Chapter 11: Slave to God, Free from Man . . . Free from God, Slave to Man

1. Morris, Benjamin F., *The Christian Life and Character of the Civil Institutions of the United States*, 145.

2. Ibid., 48.

3. Ibid., 137.

4. Ibid., 148.

5. Old Testament book of Jonah 3:6–10.

6. John F. Kennedy Presidential Library and Museum, John F. Kennedy Speeches, "The President and the Press: Address before the American Newspaper Publishers Association," April 27, 1961, accessed March 29, 2017, https://www.jfklibrary.org/Research/Research-Aids/JFK-Speeches/American-Newspaper-Publishers-Association_19610427.aspx

7. Lewis, C. S., *Mere Christianity* (New York: Macmillan Publishing Company, 1952), 36.

8. The Declaration of Independence.

9. Morris, *The Christian Life and Character*, 172.

10. Morris, 635.

11. Norris, Chuck, "The Super Bowl, the Olympics and the Best of America", Townhall.com, February 4, 2014; https://townhall.com/columnists/chucknorris/2014/02/04/the-super-bowl-the-olympics-and-the-best-of-america-n1789028

Chapter 12: Real Freedom

1. Pope John Paul II, *Message of His Holiness Pope John Paul II for the Celebration of the Day of Peace*, 1 January, 1981, "To Serve Peace, Respect Freedom," http://w2.vatican.va/content/john-paul-ii/en/messages/peace/documents/hf_jp-ii_mes_19801208_xiv-world-day-for-peace.html

2. De Tocqueville, Alexis, *Democracy in America, Volume II*, The Henry Reeve Text, rev. by Francis Bowen, ed. Phillips Bradley (New York: Alfred A. Knopf, 2001), 7.

3. Weigel, George, "A Better Concept of Freedom," *First Things*, March 2002, http://www.firstthings.com/article/2002/03/a-better-concept-of-freedom

4. Website: ushistory.org, "The Electric Franklin: The Quotable Franklin," http://www.ushistory.org/franklin/quotable/quote04.htm

5. John F. Kennedy Presidential Library and Museum, "Remarks in Nashville at the 90th Anniversary Convocation of Vanderbilt University, May 18, 1963," http://www.jfklibrary.org/Research/Research-Aids/JFK-Speeches/Vanderbilt-University_19630518.aspx

6. *Washington Post,* "Obama Extends Caps on Student Loan Payments to about Five Million People," June 9, 2014, https://www.washingtonpost.com/politics/obama-extends-caps-on-student-loan-payments-to-about-5-million-people/2014/06/09/10a6ab20-efe4-11e3-9ebc-2ee6f81ed217_story.html

Obama lashed out at congressional Republicans for opposing the Warren legislation and for voting to cut federal Pell grants, saying they were more apt to support wealthy individuals and companies than middle-class students working hard to get an education.

"If you're a big oil company, they'll go to bat for you," Obama said. "If you're a student, good luck."

Chapter 13: Is Success Our Guide?

1. Kotlikoff, Laurence, "America is Bankrupt," *Economics by Invitation, The Economist*, February 11, 2011, https://www.economist.com/comment/835362

2. Morris, *The Christian Life and Character of the Civil Institutions of the United States*, 160–161.

3. Genesis 2:24 states, " . . . a man shall leave father and mother, and shall cleave to his wife, and they shall be two in one flesh." The notes for this verse in the Douay-Rheims Bible identify the "one flesh" as the production of a child who is the blood of both.

4. Hayek, F. A., *The Road to Serfdom*, 67. Here Hayek uses a quote from Hilaire Belloc.

5. Morris, *The Christian Life and Character*, 146.

6. Ibid., 148–149.

7. Ibid.

8. Wurmbrand, Richard, *Tortured for Christ* (Bartlesville, Oklahoma: Living Sacrifice Book Company, 1998), 43.

9. Ibid.

10. Bartlett, John, and Justin Kaplan, ed., *Bartlett's Familiar Quotations, Sixteenth Edition*, (Boston: Little, Brown & Company, 1992), 701.

11. Morris, 46.

Chapter 14: Exceptionalism Is Excellence

1. Pinckaers, Servais, O. P., *The Sources of Christian Ethics*, Tr. by Sr. Mary Thomas Noble, (Washington, D.C.: The

Catholic University of America Press, 1995), 355.

2. Ibid.

3. Wurmbrand, *Tortured for Christ*, 9.

4. Sheen, Fulton J., *The Power of Love*, (New York: Simon and Schuster, Inc., 1965), 16.

5. Annals of Congress, House of Representatives, 3rd Congress, 1st Session, page 170 (1794-01-10) [10].

    The Annals summarize speeches in the third person, with the actual text of Madison's quote as follows: "Mr. Madison wished to relieve the sufferers, but was afraid of establishing a dangerous precedent, which might hereafter be perverted to the countenance of purposes very different from those of charity. He acknowledged, for his own part, that he could not undertake to lay his finger on that article in the Federal Constitution which granted a right of Congress of expending, on objects of benevolence, the money of their constituents." The expense in question was for French refugees from the Haitian Revolution.

6. De Tocqueville, Alexis, *Democracy in America*, trans. by Arthur Goldhammer, (New York: Literary Classics of the United States, 2004), 595.

7. *Catechism of the Catholic Church*, Part Three, Section One, Chapter Two, Article 1, The Communal Character of the Human Vocation, par. 1883–1894, http://www.vatican.va/archive/ccc_css/archive/catechism/p3s1c2a1.htm

8. De Tocqueville, *Democracy in America*, 593.

9. Matthew 25:14–30.

10. Cecere, Michael, "George Washington Makes The Case For a Boycott," *Journal of the American Revolution*, June 24, 2014, accessed September 29, 2016, https://allthingsliberty.com/2014/06/george-washington-makes-the-case-for-a-boycott/ (note 8)

11.   In an interview, CNBC's John Harwood asked, "When you think about something like 90 percent, you don't think that's obviously too high?" to which Sen. Bernie Sanders replied, "No." http://thinkprogress.org/economy/2015/05/26/3662773/sanders-90-percent-tax/

12.   Pope Leo XIII's encyclical "Rerum Novarum" (May 15th, 1891), paragraphs 2 and 4, http://www.papalencyclicals.net/leo13/l13rerum.htm

13.   Pope Leo XIII, "Rerum Novarum," paragraph 5.

14.   "Reply to a Committee from the Workingmen's Association of New York," March 21, 1864, Liberty & Independence Press, accessed September 29, 2016, http://www.libertyindependence.com/page/lincoln

15.   Wurmbrand, Richard, *Tortured for Christ*, 42.

16.   Summaries of each are based on the description from the website "Dante's Inferno: Seven Deadly Sins," http://www.danteinferno.info/7-deadly-sins.html

17.   Jacob, Benno, *The First Book of the Bible: Genesis*, trans. E. Jacob and W. Jacob (New York: Ktav Pub. House, 1974), 12.

    Benno Jacob was a scholarly Reform rabbi (with a University degree in Semitics) in Germany until World War II. Before leaving Germany, he produced a monumental commentary on Genesis.

Chapter 15: Exceptionalism and the Work Ethic

1.   Library of Congress, "The American Revolution, 1763-1783", Commander Washington's General Orders, July 4, 1775, accessed October 6, 2016, http://www.loc.gov/teachers/classroommaterials/presentationsandactivities/presentations/timeline/amrev/contarmy/orderone.html

Notes

2. Morris, Benjamin F., *The Christian Life and Character of the Civil Institutions of the United States,* 342.

3. The National Archives, "Founders Online," website: http://founders.archives.gov/documents/Washington/03-01-02-0358

4. "And God saw all the things that he had made, and they were very good. And the evening and morning were the sixth day." Genesis 1:31, Douay-Rheims translation.

5. *Catechism of the Catholic Church* (Washington, DC: United States Catholic Conference, Inc. 1994) 583 n. 2427.

6. http://www.theodore-roosevelt.com/images/research/speeches/trhnthopb.pdf

7. Roosevelt, Theodore, "The Strenuous Life" (10 April 1899), Voices of Democracy: The U.S. Oratory Project, University of Maryland, accessed September 29, 2016, http://voicesofdemocracy.umd.edu/roosevelt-strenuous-life-1899-speech-text/

8. http://www.ushistory.org/DECLARATION/document/ Accessed April 26, 2017.

9. Novak, Michael, *First Things,* "The Truths Americans Used to Hold, Part II: A Metaphysics of American Ideas," December 17, 2009, https://www.firstthings.com/web-exclusives/2009/12/the-truths-americans-used-to-holdpart2

10. "Noah Webster, on the Education of Youth in America," 1788, Collection 23-26, press-pubs.uchicago.edu/founders/documents/r1ch18s26.html

11. Roosevelt, Theodore, "The Strenuous Life, VII, The Eighth and Ninth Commandments in Politics," May 12, 1900, https://bartleby.com/58/7.html

12. Roosevelt, Theodore, "Lincoln and Free Speech," *Metropolitan Magazine*, New York, May 1918, Vol. 47, Number

6, pg. 7,
https://babel.hathitrust.org/cgi/pt?id=uva.x030708290&
view=1up&seq=5

Chapter 16: The Packaging

1. George Washington's Farewell Address, 1796, Yale Law
    School, Lillian Goldman Law Library, The Avalon Proj-
    ect: Documents in Law, History and Diplomacy 2008,
    http://avalon.law.yale.edu/18th_century/washing.asp

2. "So the next element of our strategy involves addressing
    the underlying grievances and conflicts that feed extrem-
    ism . . . " https://www.whitehouse.gov/the-press-
    office/2013/05/23/remarks-president-national-defense-u
    niversity

3. De Tocqueville, Alexis, *Democracy in America*, Volume
    II, 22.

4. www.history.org/almanack/life/politics/giveme.cfm

5. http://www.let.rug.nl/usa/presidents/thomas-
    jefferson/letters-of-thomas-jefferson/jefl272.php

6. Jefferson, Thomas, "Notes on the State of Virginia," ch.
    18;
    httpi//xroads.virginia.edu/~hyper/jefferson/ch18.html

7. Constitution Society,
    http://www.constitution.org/tj/ltr/1803/ltr_18030907_nic
    holas.html

8. en.wikipedia.org/wiki/America_the_Beautiful#Lyrics
    Accessed May 1, 2017.

9. https://www.merriam-webster.com/dictionary/revolution
    Accessed May 1, 2017.

10. Bartlett, John, and Justin Kaplan, ed., *Bartlett's Familiar
    Quotations*, Sixteenth Edition, (Boston, MA: Little,
    Brown & Company, 1992) p. 701.

11. Ertelt, Steven, "Shock Report Shows 98% of Babies with Down Syndrome are Aborted in Denmark," Life News.com, October 20, 2015, accessed September 29, 2016, http://www.lifenews.com/2015/10/20/shock-report-shows-98-of-babies-with-down-syndrome-are-aborted-in-denmark/

12. Amendment I (Religion), Document 69, "Joseph Story, Commentaries on the Constitution 3:§§ 1865–73," http://press-pubs.uchicago.edu/founders/documents/amendI_religions69.html, accessed May 5, 2017.

13. Morris, Benjamin F., *The Christian Life and Character of the Civil Institutions of the United States*, 157.

Chapter 17: Afloat with No Rudder

1. *Kolbe Modern History Reader*, 383.

2. From "The Gettysburg Address" delivered by Abraham Lincoln at the dedication of the Soldiers' National Cemetery in Gettysburg, Pennsylvania on November 19, 1863, during the American Civil War, four and a half months after the Battle of Gettysburg, see https://en.wikipedia.org/wiki/Gettysburg_Address#Text_of_the_Gettysburg_Address Accessed May 5, 2017.

3. Morris, Benjamin F., *The Christian Life and Character of the Civil Institutions of the United States*, 832, 833.

4. *Kolbe Modern History Reader*, 388.

5. Genesis 1:27 "And God created man to his own image: to the image of God he created him: male and female he created them."

6. Abraham Lincoln Online, Speeches and Writings, "The Gettysburg Address," Nicolay Copy, www.abrahamlincoln online.org/lincoln'speeches/Gettysburg.htm

7. *Kolbe Modern History Reader,* 388.

8. Ibid., 389.

9. Ibid.

10. Morris, *The Christian Life and Character*, 65.

11. Ibid., 183.

12. *Kolbe Modern History Reader*, 383.

13. Ibid., 387.

14. Morris, 635.

15. Ibid., 182–183.

16. Kennedy, John F., *Profiles in Courage* (New York: Harper Collins, 1964), xvii, foreword by Robert F. Kennedy.

17. Ibid.

Chapter 18: The Prodigal Nation

1. Connell, Janice T., *The Spiritual Journey of George Washington* (Janice T. Connell, 2013), 165;

   Excerpt from George Washington's Thanksgiving Proclamation, October 3, 1789, as quoted in John Frederick Schroeder's "Maxims of George Washington" (Mount Vernon, Virginia: Mount Vernon Ladies Society, 1989), 172.

2. Hardon, John A., S. J. *Modern Catholic Dictionary* (Bardstown, Kentucky: Eternal Life, 1999), 463.

3. Cato Institute, "Human Freedom Index," accessed March 8, 2019, https://www.cato.org/human-freedom-index-new

4. From the Cato Institute's report, "The Economic Freedom of the World: 2015 Annual Report," http://www.cato.org/economic-freedom-world

5. https://www.cato.org/economic-freedom-world

Notes

6.   Ibid.

7.   Morris, *The Christian Life and Character of the Civil Institutions of the United States*, 298–299.

8.   Ibid., 305.

9.   Ibid., 179.

ABOUT THE AUTHOR

FRANK MOORE IS A RETIRED FDNY LIEUTENANT. Born and raised in the Bronx, New York, Moore earned a bachelor's of science in business administration from Manhattan College. After working in banking for nearly six years in midtown Manhattan, he left the business world to become a firefighter and has never looked back. Eventually promoted to lieutenant, he was assigned to Division 6, covering the South Bronx and Harlem.

Moore has written and spoken of his experiences, 9/11, and his passion for God and country since retiring from the NYC Fire Department. He has done graduate-level work in Religious Studies at St. Joseph's Seminary in Yonkers, New York, and is a fellow of the Acton Institute in Grand Rapids, Michigan.

Made in the USA
Las Vegas, NV
11 April 2021